PERMISSION TO OFFEND

PERMISSION TO OFFEND

The Compassionate Guide
for Living Unfiltered and Unafraid

RACHEL LUNA

HarperOne
An Imprint of HarperCollinsPublishers

PERMISSION TO OFFEND. Copyright © 2023 by Rachel Luna. All rights reserved. Printed in the United States of America. No part of this book may be used or reproduced in any manner whatsoever without written permission except in the case of brief quotations embodied in critical articles and reviews. For information, address HarperCollins Publishers, 195 Broadway, New York, NY 10007.

HarperCollins books may be purchased for educational, business, or sales promotional use. For information, please email the Special Markets Department at SPsales@harpercollins.com.

FIRST EDITION

Watercolor image courtesy of Shutterstock / picgeek
Heart emoticons courtesy of Shutterstock / Turkan Rahimli

Library of Congress Cataloging-in-Publication Data has been applied for.

ISBN 978-0-06-311297-1

23 24 25 26 27 LBC 5 4 3 2 1

For my daughters, Isabella and Valentina.

And to all the #loyalLUNAtics.
May you always give yourself
Permission to Offend.

CONTENTS

PERMISSION TO OFFEND

THE MEANING OF PERMISSION TO OFFEND

I woke up to him on top of me.

"STOP! STOP!" I screamed. The room was spinning. I was completely naked, and a guy I had met only a few hours earlier was inside of me. My heart was pounding out of my chest. *What's happening? What did I do? How did I get here?* Questions raced through my mind as I tried to make sense of the moment.

"NO! Get off of me!" I screamed louder.

Looking confused, he stopped, sat up, and said, "What's wrong? I thought you wanted to. I helped you, remember?" Pushing him off of me, I got on my feet and scanned the dark room, looking for my clothes. "No! No! I didn't want this," I cried. I saw my coat on the floor but no other clothes and quickly rushed to cover up. A memory flashed in my mind as the guy repeated, "I helped you. I wasn't trying to hurt you." He *had* helped. I remembered being sick, throwing up in the bathroom, and him holding my hair back. But I didn't remember anything else. I definitely didn't remember agreeing to sleep with him.

"NO!" I cried again. "I have to go. I have to get out of here." My keys were in my coat pocket, and even though the room was still spinning, I ran for the door. When I got outside, the cold air hit my face and I sobered up for a moment. Flashes from the evening began to come together.

My coworker Juliana had invited me out for cocktails. I remember laughing when she said the word "cocktails," because even though I was a recovering alcoholic, I had never heard anyone actually use the word "cocktails" when referring to having drinks. I grew up in New York City, and over there we would have said, "Let's get lit," or, "Let's meet up for drinks." These California girls were different. I told her, "Nah, girl, I don't drink anymore. Nothing good ever happens when I drink."

"You'll be fine. We'll just have one. You can trust me. It'll be fun," she said.

Yes, I remember now. I went out for drinks with Juliana, her boyfriend, and the guy who was on top of me . . . What was his name?

Another memory flashed. This time I remembered being in the club and Juliana's boyfriend returning from the bar with two green drinks. He handed me a glass, raised his in a "Cheers" gesture, and then he made the motion to interlock his arm with mine so that I was drinking from his glass and he was drinking from mine.

The memory faded to black. *Where's my car? I need to get home.* Tears continued to fall down my face as I finally spotted my car.

It was by God's grace that I made it home safely. But the next morning, I felt like I was reliving a nightmare. I called one of my closest friends to tell her what had happened. "I think I was raped last night," I said.

"Girl, let's take you to the hospital," she said. "We have to file a police report."

"No. We can't. I work with this girl. I don't even know what happened. I was drunk, but I only remember having *one* drink. This can't be happening to me." Once again, tears began to fall.

"It doesn't matter," she insisted. "At least have them do a rape kit on you."

Taking a deep breath, I said, "Okay."

The police were dismissive, and since I couldn't remember the guy's name or the address, they said there wasn't much they could do. If I was willing to give them my coworker's name and phone number they could go after her and try to find the guy. But I refused. I was so ashamed of myself. I was so scared that everyone at work would find out. Worse, I worried that they would all say it was my fault and that I had asked for it. I left the precinct feeling worse about myself than when I'd walked in—and believe me, when I'd walked in my self-respect was at a low point.

I didn't hear a word from Juliana all weekend long, but there she was on Monday morning, front and center. "Oh my gosh, are you okay? The guys said you left crying." I just gave her a look and said, "Stay away from me." I might have believed her concern if she had called or sent a message to check on me over the weekend. But she hadn't.

I never asked Juliana for the guy's name or information. After that day she rarely spoke to me, except for the occasional work question. No "Good morning." No "Have a great weekend." Nothing.

I too remained silent. I never followed up with the police. I never tried to press charges. I just tried to pretend it had never happened.

So why would I choose silence, with Juliana, with the police, with myself? I kept silent because of the three fears we'll tackle together in this book: *judgment*, *rejection*, and *defamation*.

I was terrified of judgment from coworkers at my job and possibly in a court of law . . .

I was afraid of rejection from friends and/or partners . . .

I was afraid I would face defamation by everyone who already knew me, that they would spread ugly rumors about me. Even more terrifying, I was afraid they would use the truth of who I had been—a promiscuous alcoholic—against me for the rest of my life. So I did and said nothing.

| **DON'T CONFUSE THE TRUTH OF WHO YOU ONCE WERE WITH THE TRUTH OF WHO YOU ARE TODAY.**

#PermissiontoOffend

Maybe you haven't been sexually assaulted, but you *have* had an experience in which you did and said nothing as a means to protect yourself. Maybe this story made you think of something happening in your life right now, and you're trying to figure out if you should speak up, do something, make some kind of a change—but you're afraid your truth will offend someone. Maybe you just want to stop carrying the guilt and shame of who you *were* so you can start walking in the truth of who you *are*.

If so, this book was written for you, and my hope is that it encourages and inspires you to share the parts of your story that you have been hiding out of fear of what others might think, say, or do.

Because I know that when you start living unfiltered, unashamed, and unafraid, *your life will change!* When you start sharing *your* truth, *your* stories, and, yes, even the parts of you that have held guilt and shame, not only are you set free but others with similar stories are set free as well. No longer will you have to hide, stay silent, or reject your wants, needs, and desires for the sake of not offending others.

Let me be clear: giving yourself permission to offend is *not* about being intentionally hurtful. It's about giving yourself permission to own and share all the parts of you without the filters, the shame, or the fear that so often hold people back. Contrary to popular belief, when you give yourself permission to offend, you are not instigating conflict, division, or strife with others. It's not about saying without thinking, demanding the spotlight, or putting others down. Offending is about liberation. Truth. Empathy. Humanity. Strength of character. Character was what I had to give myself permission to build as I released a decade of shame and unworthiness. Character is what *you* might have to give yourself permission to build as you stand up for what's true for you.

When you hear the word "offend," it might bring up some stuff for you—when we think of offending others, we first think of being offended. We don't want to be one of those people who offend. I hear words like "racism," "hatred," "bigotry," "anti-vaxxer." Let me be clear: This book is not a weapon. The messages are not fuel for division. On the contrary, increasing your permission to offend increases your permission to be offended, which in turn allows others to form deeper relationships with you. There is no more loving, welcoming, inclusive, and inviting place to be than right smack-dab in the heart of this book.

After all, I've just shared one of the darkest moments of my life with you—*I'm* certainly not going to throw stones from my glass house!

When people tell me they're afraid of offending, the reality is that they're more afraid of the consequence of offense. They're worried that they might lose credibility, lose status, or even get "canceled." You're not afraid of taking action; you're afraid of what happens on the other side of action. You're afraid of being judged, rejected, and/or defamed, just like I was afraid. That is the danger zone we will be neutralizing together in this book. We are making it safe for you to do, say, and be whatever is true for you, even if it means someone is upset, annoyed, resentful, or even disgusted.

Whenever I've asked someone why they haven't spoken up or started their business, or even dyed their hair a funky color, I get a variation of the same answer: "I don't want to offend . . ." That's where it always goes, to self-rejection. You deny your own wants for the approval and acceptance of others. It's not really the fear of offending; it's the fear of how these three questions will be answered:

What will they think? (judgment)

What will they do? (rejection)

What will they tell others? (defamation)

I know you know that rejection hurts, but did you know there's a scientific explanation? According to an article published in *Psychology Today*, "the same pathways are activated when we are rejected as when we experience physical pain. This is why rejection hurts so much."* Your brain actually thinks you're being physically hurt when you experience the emotional pain of rejection. The good news is that this book will give you tools and strategies to help increase your pain tolerance.

That, along with so much more, is what you'll take away from this book. Not only will it help you release the fear attached to these three questions, but also it will help you find the courage, confidence, and strength to do and say everything you want without sacrificing what you have.

As we begin, I invite you to sign off on these four permission slips:

I give myself permission to live in truth.

I give myself permission to live in faith.

I give myself permission to live in freedom.

I give myself permission to live in abundance.

---

* Judith E. Glaser, "Why We Don't Speak Up," *Psychology Today*, May 22, 2018, https://www.psychologytoday.com/gb/blog/conversational-intelligence/201805/why-we-don-t-speak.

The book is divided into four parts based on these permission slips. By the time you finish reading this book, you will have the science-backed knowledge, tools, and strategies to help you live un-filtered, unashamed, and unafraid.

That being said, there *is* weight and responsibility associated with giving yourself *permission to offend*. Please use this work wisely. With a compassionate approach, it has the power to change the shape of our world. And oh, by the way, giving yourself permission to offend, the way I prescribe in this book, is the best way to get anything and everything you've ever wanted without losing what matters to you most. I'm living proof of this.

I, like you, have found myself in harmful patterns. One minute I had momentum, the next moment I was spiraling out of control. One day I felt fearless, ready to conquer the world, the next day I was curled up in the fetal position, hiding under my blankets. I couldn't seem to shake this feeling that something was "off" in my life, and I couldn't figure out what or why. Despite being the only one of my siblings to get a college degree, serving in the United States Marines Corps, and starting a beautiful family, I found myself at one point in my life needing to take a long hard look in the mirror. My accom-plishments were many, but I was still living in fear. I was still behav-ing counter to my own value system. I was still comparing myself to everyone around me, including family, friends, and colleagues—all of whom seemed to be passing me by. It was painful and frustrating, and more than anything, I wanted to break the cycle.

It wasn't easy and it for sure wasn't overnight. It was one small choice, one act of liberation, at a time. First, I had to get sober (again). Next, I had to reevaluate all of my relationships. I had to learn how to stop responding to certain "friends" who no longer served me. I learned how to reestablish boundaries with family members, both for my own mental health as well as for the integrity of our family. Over time, I began to not only invest in my health but also, more than that, invest in *myself.* Taking a leap of faith, I left the Marine Corps and began pursuing a career in coaching. And let me tell you, that was not easy to do at all. I was leaving the stability of a very steady paycheck with incredible benefits, lots of fun travel, as well as a tight-knit community, and entering a field that was still very new and widely criticized. People in my circle laughed when I told them I was studying to become a Certified Professional Life and Business Coach. At the time, I already had a bachelor of science in business management from Penn State University, and the next logical step would have been to get my MBA from an equally well-known university. "Why are you wasting your time becoming a life coach?!"

Knowing their questions concerning my new career path were reflections of their own fears, doubts, insecurities, and aversion to risk, I kept my head down and continued forging ahead. But I won't lie: it was hard to go against the grain and choose the road less traveled, especially when I didn't know exactly where the road would lead. Thank God for activated faith and inspired, confident action! The unpopular choices I made back then led me to *right here, right now!*

Today, a decade later, I am a Master Certified Coach with an emphasis in neuroscience coaching. I have been invited to speak on stages in Japan, Europe, and countless cities across the United States. I have been featured in *Forbes* more than once and was named one of the "11 Most Inspiring Female Entrepreneurs to Follow on Instagram." I had a full-page spread in *Latina* magazine, have been featured in *HuffPost*, and was invited by Lifetime television network's *Little Women: Atlanta* to re-create my signature event, Confidence Activated, for the show. There I was lauded as the "Confidence Coach." I have a popular podcast (also titled *Permission to Offend*) that reaches listeners in more than ninety countries worldwide, and best of all, I have literally coached tens of thousands of people all around the world. It has been a journey filled with many twists and turns, but each time I choose myself and lean into *my* truth, it continues to lead me to where God always intended me to be. The same is possible for you.

If you picked up this book, it's because you realize you have been living a watered down version of the life you want. A life that has been clouded by fear and stunted by second-guessing. A life in which you have continuously chosen the "safe" path because you were worried about what others might do or say if you trusted yourself long enough to pave your own path. That's okay! You did what you needed to do to survive. We'll talk more about that and why you needed to do that in the upcoming chapters. However, right now it is time to stop living that way.

As you read my stories and the other examples I've included, I want you to remember one thing: this is about *you*. Make no mistake, this is *not* a book to tell you what you "need" or "have" to do in order to get more of what you want. On the contrary, every word is an invitation. Each chapter offers up one or more concepts—some of which you may have heard before, others that will be new—to guide you toward connecting to the core of your personal truth. Along with that, you'll find an invitation, which I call an "alignment opportunity," and sometimes more than one; apply whatever feels most authentic and aligned for you. At the end of each chapter I've also included an affirmation to help anchor you in the lessons. Take whatever you need and ditch the rest. If you've never felt free or safe to disagree wholeheartedly with someone or something, *this is your safe space*. Go all in and feel free to cuss at me, scream at the pages, call BS, and even (which is, of course, my preference) throw your hands up and say, "Finally! Someone is saying everything I've been thinking and wanting to say."

Oh, and one more thing you should know: everything attached to me wins. Heck, if anything, it seems like most of the time anyone attached to me ends up winning even more than I do. And as my daughter Valentina says, "I am A-O-fine" with that! I'm here to see you win! Whatever winning means to you, let's go get it. Let's bring home that *W*. Just understand that many people will be offended—not that you're winning but that you had the audacity to want to play the game at all. This book will help you be A-O-fine with that! ☺

So let's get into it.

PART 1

I GIVE MYSELF PERMISSION TO LIVE IN TRUTH

Then you will know the truth, and the truth will set you free.

—JOHN 8:32, NIV

ACTIVATE YOUR TRUTH

"You're going to turn left just up ahead at the light," I said to my husband.

The tension in the air was so thick not even a butcher's knife could cut it. Earlier that morning we had gotten into a verbal scuffle with our two daughters after they both had shown up at the breakfast table with laptops in hand, barely making eye contact with us. I confess: even though there are countless books on parenting and motherhood, I didn't read a single one of them before my kids were born, and I was totally unprepared. After having suffered several miscarriages, I just always assumed I'd be so grateful to have children at all that I would cherish even the most difficult challenges of raising tiny humans. Well, that was a big fat fail of an assumption. I'm sure one day I'll look back and miss the sass and attitude from these kids, but on this particular morning, no one was cherishing anything. In fact, I was silently praying to be different from my mom because had I come to the table the way my girls had, there would have been a big "¡*Fuácata!*" (That's Puerto Rican for a smackdown.)

Nevertheless, I rose above and did my best to be a gentle, respectful parent. Apparently, that's a thing now, and I'm out here in these streets trying to break generational childhood trauma. The problem I've had to navigate throughout my life is that I am a Burden Bearer, which means I'm highly sensitive to other people's energy and emotions. So the attitude these kids were dropping was creating all sorts of tension that morning and I needed to lighten the mood. That's when I suggested we all get out of the house and check out a local fair. But this idea didn't go over well with my kids, who were annoyed at the thought of spending a day unattached to their computers. In a final act of frustration, my husband ordered us all into the car for "mandatory fun." As we piled into the vehicle, I seemed to be the only one with even an ounce of optimism, but it was dwindling fast.

> BURDEN BEARER: ONE WHO HAS THE CAPACITY TO EMPATHIZE, SHARE, AND SHOULDER THE EMOTIONAL LOADS OF OTHERS.
> BEING A BURDEN BEARER IS A GIFT THAT CAN BE BOTH POSITIVE AND NEGATIVE.

I sat in the front seat with my phone in hand, watching the GPS arrow inch closer to the left while our car rolled along in the center lane. Growing antsy, I said a little more forcefully, "Babe . . . left. Just up ahead." Radio silence. No acknowledgment whatsoever from my husband. It was fine if he didn't feel like talking to me, but our vehicle hadn't moved an inch toward the left. We were going to miss the turn. Trying my hardest not to lose my cool, I gave one final yet stern effort: "The GPS says we need to turn left here." All the muscles in my neck were working overtime as I tried hard not to break with my positive attitude.

Nothing. Not a single utterance. No movement of the steering wheel or acknowledgment of anything I had just said, and that, my friend, is when I lost it.

"Why do you do this? I know you hear me!"

I was so pissed that I can't be 100 percent certain if my husband acknowledged me or not. But I do remember yelling, "You know what? Forget it! Let's just go home." He jerked the wheel, cutting off the car behind us, whipped my silver Honda Accord around, and stepped on the gas toward our home. *Oh, so now you wanna turn left?* I began cursing my husband out in my head. You should have heard me. Ooh, I told him all about himself. *So now you wanna drive like an ass and tailgate? I hope you get a ticket! Where are the cops when you need them? Always thinking you know better than me. And don't even try to talk to me when we get home because I don't want to hear anything you have to say. Okay? Okay!*

Mind you, I said none of that. I just sat quietly in the car. I'm surprised my tongue wasn't bleeding as I bit down to stay silent. In my mind, I was alternating between cursing him out and praying for God to give me peace and the patience to keep my mouth shut. When we pulled into our driveway about fifteen minutes later, I got out of the car, passive-aggressively slammed my door shut, and called my girls to follow me into the house. Rather than joining us, my husband peeled out of our driveway to go who knows where. This was common practice for us both. Driving to clear our heads is our default, so I wasn't surprised or concerned when he left. If anything, I felt relieved. You know that feeling? Something happens with someone you care about, things go off the rails, and although you want to work it out, you're momentarily grateful they're nowhere in your space. Effectively, you've been saved from yourself and the many other ways you might lash out and make things worse.

As I collected myself, I wondered how a pretty Saturday morning had turned into such a major fiasco.

All I had wanted to do was get the girls out of the house and do something together as a family. What was there to be upset about? After all, we live the "American dream" in a home with a pool. On a golf course. We have two beautiful daughters and a Maltipoo puppy named Layla. Both my husband and I had come such a long way, me growing up in New York City and him coming from a border town in Mexico. We had "made it." With everything we had, we should have been waking up every single day feeling joy and gratitude, actually looking forward to being together. What the heck was going on? How had this become my life—again?

This wasn't the first time my husband and I hadn't seen eye to eye. In fact, after nearly a decade of marriage, I struggled to remember a time—if ever such a time existed—when we were on the exact same page. Instead, our relationship had been one of loneliness and isolation, with an occasional high point during some sort of vacation or adventure. I only ever saw my own loneliness, but as we fought for our marriage, I discovered I wasn't the only one who felt alone in the relationship. There were moments when we each started to give up. One of us would toss our hands in the air and proclaim we were done, while the other silently prayed and asked God for a miracle.

It seemed like we were two ships passing in the night—until one January evening, when we finally got our miracle. As we held hands at a church revival, the pastor said, "If you came here for a breakthrough, don't leave this building until you get it." When the pastor made the final altar call—the cue for general dismissal—my husband got up to leave, but I grabbed his hand and squeezed. Looking up at him, I said, "We haven't gotten our breakthrough, and I'm not leaving until we do." That night, something changed for us both. I like to think that seeing my commitment to our marriage is what softened my husband's heart. But deep down, I think it was a God thing. After praying together through tear-filled eyes, we left the building with our breakthrough. From that moment we had compassion for each other's shortcomings—something that previously had been void in our relationship—and a renewed sense of commitment to each other.

It was as though a weight had been lifted off our shoulders. Suddenly we were a team, because that night it wasn't just me fighting for him or him fighting for me, it was *we* fighting for *us*. We knew we loved each other; we just needed to learn *how* to love each other again. Ironically, it didn't mean figuring out how to be kinder to each other. We both needed to learn how to give ourselves permission to offend so that we could have honest conversations that are sometimes difficult but so incredibly necessary.

You know, the kind of honest conversations that should be had the first time you suspect something is off in your relationship. The kind of honest conversations you should have so that all your questions can be answered and you can make the best informed decisions for yourselves. The kind of honest conversations that you've been thinking about having but just haven't had the courage to go through with.

I truly believe that if I had known the principles covered in this book sooner, perhaps we could have avoided much of the heartache and pain in those early years of marriage. But maybe we weren't ready then. It's often said the teacher appears when the student is ready. And even when we do learn, we don't always implement what we learn. I hope today is your "ready" day and that reading this book helps you have that one honest conversation you've been holding out on having.

After our breakthrough and up until that Saturday morning, things had been going great for my husband and me. But as I heard the car's engine grow more distant as he drove away, I felt a twinge of panic wash over me. This was definitely one of those knowing-better-but-not-doing-better moments for us.

I wasn't able to connect the dots at the time, but the source of stress that morning wasn't the left turn. It was that, at my core, I was afraid of being rejected. It's the fear of *rejection* that holds us back so often in life, from things like asking for a raise, starting a business, or, in my case at this moment, speaking up and challenging both my children and my husband. Deep down inside, a part of me believed that if I spoke up about what I was feeling, I would be rejected. This belief had developed over years as a result of negative thought patterns. As you're about to witness, our thoughts—at least our initial thoughts—can't always be trusted.

TRUE-ISH

Have you heard the popular cognitive behavioral therapy concept that states, "Your thoughts create your feelings"? That phrase gets tossed around a lot, and it always irritates me. I mean, it's true, but only true-*ish*. It's not *just* the thoughts that create the feelings. It's the *story* that leads to the feelings. And even that isn't entirely true. It's the story as well as the meaning we assign to the story. The Stoic philosopher Epictetus said it best: "Man [or, in this case, people of all genders] is troubled not by events but by the meaning he [she/they] gives them." Let's look again at the example from earlier. I wasn't upset that my husband didn't turn left. I was upset because I was making his refusal to merge left mean something about me.

I thought, *He's not listening to me.* But the meaning I assigned was that he didn't care about what I had to say. I then told myself the story that my husband didn't care about what I had to say because he thought I was stupid. And way, way, way down in the depths of my subconscious, in that dark place many of us never want to enter, were the most terrifying stories of all. *They're all going to reject me. He thinks I'm stupid and he's going to leave me. My kids want nothing to do with me. I'm not even good enough for my own family.*

Now, listen. I *know* none of those stories are true, but those thoughts existed somewhere in me. They exist within all of us in some form or another. The more I replayed the scene in my mind, the more vivid the stories became in my head, and the angrier I grew. Ever been in a similar situation? One thing happens and it totally sends you into a tailspin. I used to think this was just a by-product of being a Puerto Rican girl from New York City, but no. Even white girls from the suburbs are guilty of letting their stories send them into table-flipping rages. Through my studies in neuroscience coaching, I learned that all human beings go through this because we are unable to control the vast majority of our thoughts. And speaking of thoughts, what the hell is a thought anyway?

A *thought* is defined as a mental representation of something. Scientists have varying theories as to why and how thoughts form in the brain, but universally they agree that most thoughts happen automatically. That's what you need to remember moving forward: Most thoughts happen automatically. You can't control them! At least not at first. From our automatic thoughts come stories, which are sometimes automatic too. Other times, our stories are intentionally assigned after we've taken the time to process the situation.

Okay, so what's a story? I'm glad you asked.

A *story* is an account of events based on our thoughts, perceptions, experiences, and beliefs.

If you're a notetaker like I am, now would be the time to grab your highlighter and highlight this:

The stories we tell ourselves are neutral. They are neither good nor bad. Like Epictetus said, it's the *meaning* we assign stories that categorizes them as good or bad. The feelings that accompany the assigned meaning influence how we respond.

WHAT DOES IT MEAN?

Where does meaning come from, anyway?

The meaning we assign to our stories is derived from our beliefs, programming, and experiences.

We believe one plus one equals two, saying "Please" and "Thank you" means you're polite, and the little girl who is decisive on the playground is bossy—because that's what we are taught in school. Just as our beliefs are initially imposed on us, some of our stories can also be imposed by our primary caregivers, teachers, and leaders. Now, I can already hear someone saying, "No, Rachel, one plus one equals two because that's basic math." I hear you, boo. We'll get to facts in just a minute, but for now, just go with me.

Picture it: 2000-something. A young, early twenties me calls my mom to tell her I have been diagnosed with bipolar disorder, anxiety, and depression all in one therapy session. My psychologist at the time had prescribed three different mood stabilizers, or as I referred to them: an upper, a downer, and an in-betweener. My mom immediately snaps, "You don't need that. Don't let them put you on any medication." Her usually well-masked Spanish accent begins to poke through, as it often does when she's agitated. "You are strong, Rachel," she continues, before breaking into Spanish to add, "*No se lo digas a nadie.* (Don't tell anyone.)" Can you imagine?! Instantly, I feel both shame and relief. Shame because I interpret my mom's request to keep this info to myself to mean there is something wrong with me. And relief because she is so convinced I don't need medication that I'm able to open myself up to the possibility that maybe I don't need it. This really happened and I thought, *Either she's crazy or I'm crazy, but one of us is for sure crazy.*

Looking back, it's easy for me to see how my fear of rejection was anchored—which is another way of saying cemented or ingrained—by my mother telling me to keep the diagnosis to myself. I can see how I would have subconsciously interpreted her appeal for my secrecy to mean that telling others would result in my rejection. After all, she had just rejected my diagnosis, and in my mind, this was the same as her having rejected *me*. This went on to plant a seed in the back of my mind, creating a fear of rejection that would pop up again and again throughout my life. Can you relate? What, if anything, has come up for you so far? Can you recall a seemingly insignificant moment in your life that, as you reflect now, actually triggered the fear of rejection that you might still be carrying?

That conversation with my mom and the story I created from it confirms what science has already proven. Both our beliefs and stories can be influenced at any time, and at any age. This is why, as you'll see in chapter 2, defining an identity is so important. When your identity is defined, you're less influenced or impressed by the stories and beliefs of others and more driven by the desires of your heart and soul.

Looking back now, if I had known then how to do the work I'm about to invite you to do in just a moment, I would have compassionately challenged my mom. I would have asked her what my diagnosis meant to her. I would have asked her to share what she was afraid might happen if I told others. And I certainly would have told her that it was okay for her to not understand my choices. But alas, hindsight is 20/20. My almost daily chats with my mom are much different now, and I hope your conversations following this book shift as well.

So let's keep going, because there's one other thing you need to know about thoughts, stories, and meaning.

SLOW YOUR SCROLL

Consider this: Have you ever been scrolling through social media and a few minutes later found yourself in a bad mood? You're not sure what happened, but all of a sudden you feel pretty "meh." Chances are, you were telling yourself a story in the background.

Perhaps you saw a post from someone celebrating a major milestone, like receiving a promotion at work or hitting a major revenue goal in their business. Consciously, you didn't think much of it, but seeing the celebration triggered a subconscious thought about your own career path or business and the lack you have in that area. You tell yourself a story about why they're winning and you're not. Almost automatically and most definitely unconsciously, you attach meaning to that story—that you're inadequate and not good enough—and lo and behold, you have a "meh" feeling upon clicking away from that media. You proceed to let a bad mood carry you through the day with loved ones and colleagues.

This is the story loop:

ACTION ⟶ THOUGHT ⟶ MEANING ⟶

FEELING/EMOTION ⟶ BEHAVIOR ⟶ ACTION/EVENT

Because thoughts are automatic, we can't do a lot to curb those. But we can influence the stories we tell ourselves about our thoughts, and especially the meaning we assign to those stories. That's where we have the power to keep from turning a simple scroll on social media into a bad mood that lasts all day or even all week! (P.S. This sort of negative story loop is also the kind of thing that keeps you stuck and failing to take action on your goals and dreams.) The good news is that not all story loops are negative. The even better news is that you can do something about the negative loops, which I'm about to show you.

ALIGNMENT OPPORTUNITY

The next time you find yourself roaming on social media, pay attention to how you feel and challenge those emotions. Ask yourself the following questions:

What am I feeling?

Why do I feel this way?

When was the last time I didn't feel this way?

What did I see?

What did I think?

What story did I tell myself?

Sure, you don't have to open the app in the first place—that's also a great opportunity to notice the influence you have on your life. But sometimes (like my husband turning left!) the action that initiates the story loop is out of your control. So the key is knowing how to keep a close account of this loop at work, and break it when necessary.

The story loop concept isn't a Rachel Luna original, although I would love to take full credit because it's so damn good. In reality, I've adapted Dr. Albert Ellis's model and added my own little *sazón* to it. The story loop looks a little something like this:

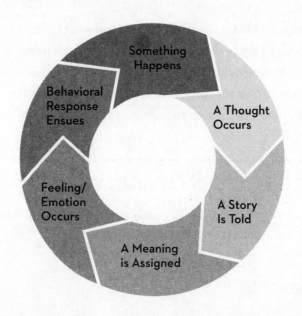

SOMETHING HAPPENS ⟶ YOU HAVE A THOUGHT ⟶ YOU TELL
YOURSELF A STORY (CONSCIOUSLY OR NOT) ⟶ YOU MAKE
THAT STORY MEAN SOMETHING (CONSCIOUSLY OR NOT) ⟶ YOU HAVE
A FEELING (THIS MAY HAPPEN BEFORE YOU ARE CONSCIOUSLY
AWARE OF YOUR THOUGHTS) ⟶ YOU HAVE A CONSCIOUS
RESPONSE OR AN UNCONSCIOUS REACTION ⟶ SOMETHING ELSE
HAPPENS AND THE LOOP CONTINUES.

Dr. Ellis's original ABC model (actions, beliefs, consequences) doesn't take into account that our thought patterns are what reinforce our beliefs. Expanding his model helps us have a better understanding of what's going on in our minds.

Although this typical pattern illustrates a conscious story, it is entirely possible—as was just described in the social media example—to first experience awareness of your feelings and emotions before you realize a story is being replayed in your mind. Throughout it all, the brain is doing what it was designed to do: make meaning. I don't want to turn this into a major dissertation on the brain, but I find it helpful and somewhat soothing to know there is a scientific explanation for many of our behaviors. The brain is wired for survival. It looks for patterns in our thoughts and behaviors to create automations that help with efficiency. One primary survival tool is our ability to understand one another, but in order to understand others, we must first understand ourselves. That's why I love studying how the brain works, and I will sprinkle in little tidbits here and there throughout this book. Because #themoreyouknow.

To further illustrate, here's a breakdown of what my own story loop looked like using the example I shared earlier about my husband.

SOMETHING HAPPENED.	My husband didn't acknowledge me or turn left at my direction.
I HAD A THOUGHT.	We're going to miss the turn.
I TOLD MYSELF A STORY.	He never listens to me.
I ASSIGNED MEANING TO MY STORY.	He's not listening because he thinks I'm stupid.
I HAD FEELINGS.	I felt angry, hurt, and rejected.
I REACTED TO MY STORY.	I had an emotional outburst and insisted we go home.

Looking at this, I'm reminded of how my story *No one listens to me* has looped over and over, on repeat, not just with my husband but also with other relationships in my life. I've often lamented, *My kids don't listen to me.* Maybe you haven't had any of the thoughts I've had, but can you think of your own story loop? When was the last time things didn't go as planned? What is something you've wanted to do but haven't been able to take action or follow through on? When did you hold yourself back from speaking up? Come on, I know you've got something.

Fill in the story loop below. Be as detailed as possible. We often miss the value by staying vague.

WHAT HAPPENED?

WHAT DID YOU THINK?

WHAT STORY DID YOU TELL YOURSELF?

WHAT DID YOU MAKE IT MEAN?

WHAT DID YOU FEEL?

WHAT WAS YOUR RESPONSE OR REACTION?

Now reflect on these questions:

What did you notice as you filled in the story loop?

Can you see a thought pattern or story that's shown up repeatedly in your life?

Is there a trend in your emotions?

Often, in an attempt to "stay positive," we try to disregard the feelings produced by these unconscious stories. This in turn can leave us feeling heavy, sad, unmotivated, or other low-energy vibrations.

However, in order to live in the freedom of being the most fully self-expressed version of yourself, you (I, we) have to pay attention to these little triggers and sudden onsets of "meh" or other seemingly unexplained emotions. When you do so, you might just discover that you're feeling inadequate, "behind," or, as one client put it, "underachieving," not because that's the fact of your life but because you told yourself a story that doesn't serve you.

—————— ENCOURAGEMENT ——————

DON'T WORRY IF YOU CAN'T THINK OF SOMETHING ON THE SPOT. IT'S NORMAL TO FEEL SOME RESISTANCE FROM TIME TO TIME. FOLD THE BOTTOM CORNER OF THIS PAGE AND MAKE A NOTE TO COME BACK TO IT. DO THIS WHENEVER YOU FIND YOURSELF STUCK ON AN EXERCISE, AND MAKE AN AGREEMENT WITH YOURSELF TO COME BACK AND COMPLETE IT.

———————————————————— #PermissiontoOffend ———

WHAT'S YOUR STORY?

Let me tell you this: no matter what your life has been like up to this point, I assure you, you've got a story. Most likely you have many stories. Potentially even more frightening: you've got an underlying belief that the story you haven't wanted to admit exists—is actually true. *Yikes!* I get it. I cringe every time I think of my own stories and beliefs. But I've worked with hundreds of clients, from every walk of life, and my favorites are the ones who tell me, "I don't have a story. I've lived a pretty uneventful life. I'm not that interesting." When my clients finally start getting honest with themselves, when they stop saying, "I already know that," and actually surrender to do the work, there's always a story. The people who end up getting the biggest breakthroughs and experience the greatest transformations are those who are willing to confront the fears they've so desperately tried to overcome.

Spoiler alert: you can't overcome a fear you're not willing to face.

Your mission is to reach the point of awareness and keep going. Results require action, and it's your turn to do the work.

FRAMEWORK FOR FREEDOM

That Saturday, instead of continuing to stew in my anger and frustration over my husband and the left turn he didn't take, I invested my time in trying to understand what had transpired from breakfast to the moment I heard my husband drive off on his own. I took myself through the very same process I take my clients through when something isn't working in their lives. I want to take you through that process now.

STEP 1: ACKNOWLEDGE THE STORY LOOP. Awareness is critical. If you don't recognize and acknowledge that you're in a loop, you won't be able to change anything. And the desires you have to improve your life will be left unfulfilled. In other words, you'll be stuck like chuck, and I know you don't want that!

STEP 2: IDENTIFY THE FACTS. This step is absolutely necessary for freedom. Separate the facts of what happened from the story, or stories, you have of the event. This allows you to create an entirely new experience, not only in relation to the people around you but also in the most important relationship of all: the relationship you have with yourself.

I learned the concept of separating facts from stories at a personal development seminar several years ago. The facilitators spent three days helping participants work through this process, but this Framework for Freedom shortens that journey. When I take my clients through this, they experience breakthroughs in as little as twenty minutes. I've shortened the gap for you so that when you feel insecure and full of doubt, you can walk through this process quickly and step into the highest version of yourself. You know, the version of yourself that's ready to take on the world but has stayed mostly in the background? *That you.*

———— IDENTIFY THE FACTS ————————————

THIS IS KEY TO CREATING AN ENTIRELY NEW EXPERIENCE WITH THE MOST IMPORTANT RELATIONSHIP OF ALL: YOUR RELATIONSHIP WITH YOURSELF.

————————————————————— #PermissiontoOffend ——

Take action now, and remember there isn't just one fact or one story you need to assess. As you go through this book, I encourage you to look at every aspect of your life and uncover the stories and facts of each situation—both in the past and in the present. Areas like money, health, relationships, and even dreams that you've long given up on.

For now, choose one specific event. Identify the story and separate the facts.

What happened?

What's the story?

The fact is:

The fact is:

The fact is:

Here's an example of how my client Jenn completed this step. Jenn runs a profitable online business with the hopes of building it into a mini empire. By most standards, she is "successful," and yet even she has stories that are holding her back. Let's take a look.

WHAT HAPPENED?

I'm just not showing up. I've worked on visibility so much over the last several years and felt like I was showing up more and more, and then, as my business has up-leveled, I unconsciously started hiding again. WTF? At this point, I am a multi-six-figure business owner. I have big financial goals. And now, as I'm working toward it, I'm hiding again. At first it was "I'm way too busy with client work to do it." Then it was "I don't want to do it." So I opened up my schedule a bit. And I hired an amazing social media manager who writes in my voice really well. But I still need to show up and create stories and reels and go live. And I'm just not doing it. Why?

WHAT'S THE STORY?

Being more visible means I'm going to be judged more. It takes so much work and so much time. I'll be judged and people won't like me or will think I'm a fraud. Plus, I see how other successful people are judged, and I don't want to be judged or talked about. And visibility takes a lot of work and too much time.

THE FACT IS:

I'm a multi-six-figure business owner.

THE FACT IS:

I like people to like me and I want to be liked. I don't want to be judged.

THE FACT IS:

Other successful people are judged. The other successful people that I see being judged have achieved a lot of what I want to achieve.

THE FACT IS:

It does take time. The amount of time I spend on visibility is up to me.

Can you spot the recurring stories in Jenn's example? I noticed that her fear of judgment was the major player in her story. Her concern around how much time showing up would cost her also stuck out to me.

Now it's your turn. If you're like me, you skipped the work and went straight to Jenn's story because you like examples. So now that you saw her example in action, it's time for you to get into action. Remember, things don't improve or stay the same if you do nothing—they get worse! So give yourself a fighting chance and do something.

Yay! You did it (or so I'm telling myself). Now look at the difference between your story and the facts. Pretty powerful, right? Now that you have this skill, you can use it going forward to break down any stories that come up and examine them by simply saying, "The fact is . . ." Then think about and/or write down what actually happened. Not how it made you feel. Not what you thought it meant. Not what you thought the other person was trying to do. Just the facts.

STEP 3. QUESTION THE STORY. Once you've identified and separated the story, or stories, it's time to question them. Validate or disprove each story by asking yourself these questions:

Is this true?

What evidence do I have to validate or disprove this story?

Is my evidence rational or irrational?

Here's how Jenn responded to step 3:

IS THIS TRUE?

Will I be judged? Yes.

Will everyone like me? No

WHAT EVIDENCE DO I HAVE TO VALIDATE OR DISPROVE THIS STORY?

People judge. But that's their own shit that they have to work through.

Even when I'm hiding there are still people who don't like me. Being more visible doesn't change that. And I don't need everyone to like me.

I'm not for everyone. I don't need thousands of clients. For my one-on-one ads services, I can take on only so many people.

Oooh. Did you see that shift? We're not even done with the Framework for Freedom and already Jenn's thoughts and attitude are shifting. Can you see how she removed her filter and declared that any judgment from others was their own stuff to work through? Also, did you notice how she was unashamed and unafraid to declare that she's not for everyone? Brava, Jenn!

Now you try it. Get your own shift right here, right now.

| THE KEY TO CLARITY IS CURIOSITY.

#PermissiontoOffend

The key to clarity is curiosity.* The more curious you get about what you're experiencing in your day-to-day life and identify the thought, feeling, and story behind the events, the quicker you'll move onto a new path to emotional freedom. Part of the reason we don't speak up sooner, or hold ourselves back from doing things that align with our desires, is because we're trapped in cul-de-sacs of confusion. This is why I encourage you to take advantage and complete each alignment opportunity offered in this book. I know how easy

---

* Quote source unknown. Not a "Rachel Luna" original.

it can be to skip ahead and tell yourself you'll come back to it later. But if you want clarity and connection to your truth, then it's worth taking the time to do the work *now*.

STEP 4. CHOOSE YOUR BELIEF. Remember, most of your thoughts are automatic, but did you also know that many of your automatic thoughts are the product of your core beliefs? In a bit, we'll delve deeper into core beliefs and the important role they play in giving you permission to offend, but right now here's what you need to know to complete this step of the Framework for Freedom:

Beliefs are a *choice*. A fascinating article in the *Indian Journal of Psychiatry* on *"The Biochemistry of Belief,"* states, "We have the power to choose our beliefs. Our beliefs become our reality."* Once you've completed the first three steps of the Framework for Freedom, you get to choose what you want to believe moving forward.

This reminds me of one of my clients, Danielle. She came to me because she was struggling to build her business and was afraid of something she couldn't put her finger on. Every time she would get a bit of momentum, something would happen to take the wind out of her sails (and sales!—pun intended). She was stuck in this cycle of false starts, and it was crushing her soul.

During one of our sessions she remembered something from her childhood. It was her brother's fourth birthday, and when it came time to cut the cake, Danielle's mom had sliced it unevenly. No big deal, right? There was just one problem. Her brother got a bigger slice, and to Danielle, who was only eight at the time, this was a *huge* deal. As she recounted the story to me, I asked, "How did that make you feel?"

"Like I wasn't good enough. Like she loved him more than she loved me," she replied. Prior to that session, Danielle hadn't been able to put her finger on why, growing up, she never felt good

---

* T. S. Sathyanarayana Rao, M. R. Asha, K. S. Jagannatha Rao, and P. Vasudevaraju, "The Biochemistry of Belief," *Indian Journal of Psychiatry* 51, no. 4 (2009): 239–41, https://www.ncbi.nlm.nih.gov/pmc/articles/PMC2802367/.

enough. As an eight-year-old who had just been given a smaller slice of cake, Danielle decided right then and there that her parents loved her brother more than they loved her. He was special. She was insignificant. In her mind, Danielle had to work harder to prove her worth to her parents.

This was a defining moment that created a story Danielle would repeatedly tell herself. This narrative would shape her mind and actions for more than a decade. When a friendship would end, a job opportunity would fall through, or a disagreement with her spouse came up, Danielle would immediately go back to her story of not being good enough. That is, until she learned how to work through the Framework for Freedom.

After completing these steps, Danielle had to make a choice. She could choose to continue believing her parents loved her brother more than they loved her, or she could choose to believe her mom had just sliced the cake unevenly and that was all.

Although new beliefs don't become automatic thoughts overnight, with time and reinforcement they can take hold and help you create a new reality. Eventually the road runs out and you will either do the work or continue to let fear win. Danielle chose the former—to do the work—and it completely changed her life for the better.

Returning to Jenn's example, in case you were wondering how that turned out, here's how her curiosity helped her complete step 4 of the Framework for Freedom, and choose her belief:

What people think of me is none of my business. I want to show up and be vulnerable. I want to show up more.

I'm deciding to energetically show up more and be visible.

I believe that when I show up as who I am, the right people will want to work with me.

She also addressed the idea that it would take time:

> Yes, creating content takes time. Can I plan the time? Yeah, I can schedule it out. Can I also hire help to plan that out more and make it easier? Yup.

After completing the Framework for Freedom around her visibility story, Jenn told me this work helped her to *decide* to show up and be more visible again. She said, "This is huge. I haven't been willing to be visible for months. Now I am."

I wonder what you'll decide to do after you set yourself free.

THE ACTIVATION OF TRUTH

Unfortunately, and often to our detriment, we sometimes confuse truth with fact.

A *fact* is something that cannot be argued.

The *truth* can include facts but is also influenced by beliefs and perception.

This is why we can see two sides of the same argument. Perception influences reality.

We consistently tell stories that support our beliefs and call it truth. But are these truths fact? Sometimes yes, sometimes no. More important, ask yourself this: *Are the stories I've created around the facts of my life serving me or hurting me?* Let's go back to Danielle and the piece of cake. The story Danielle told herself about it negatively affected her life for more than a decade. She frequently battled feelings of unworthiness. It was this story that held her back from starting her business and creating the financial stability and freedom she craved for her family. In her case, Danielle's story hurt her more than the events themselves.

On the other hand, some stories serve us. Take Nicole, for example.* As a young child, Nicole had undiagnosed attention deficit disorder. She was restless in school and constantly felt frustrated. The restlessness and frustration were facts. One day after watching a movie about a child who was an autistic genius, Nicole decided she too was an autistic genius. That was the story she told herself about her restlessness and frustration. When her teachers suggested Nicole's parents put her on medication, Nicole refused. She rejected the diagnosis, insisting to her parents she didn't have ADD. Instead, she chose to believe her own story about her symptoms: she was an autistic genius. She made it through elementary, middle, and high schools without any medication, and to this day, Nicole continues to navigate life without any prescription drugs. She is high functioning and runs a seven-figure business. Although she no longer insists she is an autistic genius, Nicole was able to leverage the story that served her best. Thanks to that story, she learned how to work *with* her attention deficit disorder rather than see it as a hindrance. That was her activating her truth.

Permission Slip

I give myself permission to amplify the stories that serve me best.

#PermissiontoOffend

You have the same opportunity to activate your truth when you *choose* the stories you want to believe. The Framework for Freedom we just went through helps you do just that. As you amplify those stories,

---

* Some names have been changed for privacy.

you'll begin to notice the shift in your confidence and, by extension, *your life*.

SENSITIVITY CHECK: As someone who has been diagnosed with both attention deficit disorder and anxiety, I know firsthand how mental health and associated medications can be stigmatized. I am neither for nor against anyone taking whatever they need to function at their peak performance. By sharing Nicole's story, my intention is to illustrate two things: (1) how a story can serve you, and (2) how powerful the mind can be once it chooses to believe a story. That being said, if you are currently taking medications, please do not attempt to get off your meds without consulting your physician.

Remember, you're learning the *Permission to Offend* way of living, and as such, you can rest in the comfort of knowing that ADD, anxiety disorder, depression, perfectionism, or anything else you may have struggled with only means whatever you make it mean.

FACING MY OWN FACTS

As I reflected on everything that had transpired that Saturday morning between my husband and me, it was easy to see how ignoring my feelings and subtle subconscious nudges had led to my outburst.

My storytelling had begun that morning when the kids brought their laptops to the table. (At the time, we didn't allow our children to have phones, so they would lug their laptops to our table.) My babies, engrossed in their screens, barely acknowledged my husband or me during breakfast. We were both upset by this, but neither one of us wanted to be the bad cop and tell the kids to get off their devices to be present with the family. Especially when both of us were chronically guilty of being on our phones way too much. That was the first nudge.

We said nothing, but we felt a lot of conflicting emotions. I was telling myself a story that I was a bad mom for letting the kids use their computers at the table. This one story was the start of an avalanche of negative emotions as the morning progressed. How often have you felt something but dismissed it because you didn't want to make a big deal, and especially because you felt like you didn't have enough of a leg to stand on?

When I suggested we leave the house and head to the fair, the kids did what typical preteens do: they complained and begged to stay home so they could play with their friends. I can't speak for my husband, but I can tell you I felt both rejected by my children and angry with myself for not having set stronger boundaries around electronics from the get-go. Again, I was telling myself stories about the kind of parent I was. As the subconscious stories carried on, my emotions continued to rise. But rather than acknowledge them, I continued to suppress.

It looked a little something like this:

SOMETHING HAPPENED.	The kids came to the breakfast table with their laptops, barely acknowledging us.
I HAD A THOUGHT.	I don't want to be the bad cop who tells them to put away their devices.
I TOLD MYSELF A STORY.	We're missing precious moments with the kids.
I ASSIGNED MEANING TO MY STORY.	Letting my kids use their electronics at the table means I'm a bad mom.
I HAD FEELINGS.	I felt sadness, anger, frustration, rejection.
I REACTED TO MY STORY.	I sought connection by suggesting we leave the house and go to the fair.

The loop continued:

SOMETHING HAPPENED.	The kids complained at the suggestion of leaving the house.
I HAD A THOUGHT.	I don't understand why everything is such a fight with these girls.
I TOLD MYSELF A STORY.	All they do is hide or complain instead of wanting to be with us.
I ASSIGNED MEANING TO MY STORY.	I'm failing as a mom.
I HAD FEELINGS.	I felt disappointment, frustration, rejection.
I REACTED TO MY STORY.	Emotion (conscious or unconscious) was repressed and resentment began to brew.

Remember just a little bit ago when we were using the example of social media scrolling, and I encouraged you to get curious about your emotions? This is why. Often things that seem minor become the agitators that manifest into something major.

As I contemplated all that had transpired, I recognized that it was the sum of all these little stories, plus the final straw of my husband not turning left, that added up to my explosive reaction. Once I was able to gain that perspective, it took so much volatility out of the situation. I wish I could tell you that by identifying the facts, all ended well with my husband when he returned from his drive. But that's not exactly how it went down. You see, I didn't complete the entire Framework for Freedom. I stopped at step 2 and didn't bother to question my stories or choose new beliefs.

Here's what actually happened: Upon his return, my husband immediately sequestered himself in our bedroom. Although I had identified the facts from my stories, I hadn't yet fully processed the root of my anger. In my typical, hot-tempered Latina way, I stormed into the room and said, "Hey! I'm telling myself stories about what happened today, and I need to know which one is true. The stories I'm telling myself are that you think I'm stupid and you don't care what I have to say. Is this true? Do you think I'm stupid, or do you just not care about anything I have to say?" I looked at him impatiently as he lay on our bed, looking both surprised and irritated.

"Well, first of all," he said matter-of-factly, "you *are* telling yourself stories, and both of them are wrong."

In previous years, this exchange would have quickly escalated, with both of us reacting with lots of passive-aggressive activities, like slamming doors or taking our frustrations out on dirty dishes. Nothing like an argument to get a house cleaned. *Am I right?*

Instead, my husband met my anger with patience and a level of emotional intelligence I had not seen in him before. He was right. I was telling myself stories and none of them were true. Had I taken the time to complete the framework, I could have disproved my stories.

"This isn't the first time this has happened. I feel like a lot of times I say something to you and you don't acknowledge me, and especially when we're in the car, you never listen to me even when I tell you what the GPS is saying. I feel like you think I'm stupid," I explained.

Over the next forty-five minutes, my husband and I were able to have an open, honest, and meaningful conversation. This was the kind of intimacy and connection I had craved years earlier at the start of our marriage but that I had avoided because I was so afraid to come across as a nagging wife. I didn't want to rock the boat. So instead, I just let my silence and resentment weigh us down to the point of almost causing us to sink.

The conversation on that Saturday evening ended with us snuggling up in bed and enjoying a teen-like make-out session. Identifying the facts led to activating love and compassion.

The reason my husband and I were able to navigate through that Saturday morning experience and end up kissing and cuddling in bed is that we were both willing to identify our stories as well as give ourselves permission to offend the other person while standing in our individual truths. Facing my fear of rejection by doing the thing I thought would push him away (being unapologetic about how I was feeling and communicating that frustration) was the thing that actually brought us together.

I've seen many people, not just women, deny their own feelings in order to not rock the boat. They'll make excuses or vow to speak up when there's "a better time." Sure, this might buy you some momentary peace, but ultimately it just makes things worse. As hurt and resentment continue to build, the burdens pile up. At the end of the day, what remains is a fractured relationship, in which each party is limited from fully realizing their personal potential and that of their relationship. Is that what you want? To feel stifled and unfulfilled? I don't think so. You've been called to a higher standard by virtue of the fact that your soul led you here. I don't believe in coincidences, only divine appointments. You might be scared, but you're ready to do the scary things that you might have avoided before because you were worried what other people might think or feel or how they might respond. I hope, as we continue on this journey together, the stories I share will inspire you to take action, do the exercises in each chapter, and give yourself permission to offend. If you've ever had a physical adjustment, taken a stretching class, or done other body alignment work, you know it isn't always easy, but the freedom that follows sure is worth the temporary discomfort.

I suspect if I had taken the time to complete the entire Framework for Freedom and chosen a new belief, our bedroom convo might not have been as explosive as it initially was. But hey, hopefully me taking one for the team inspires you to never skip a step, no matter how justified you might feel in the moment.

BEAUTY BEWARE, RESISTANCE IS UP AHEAD

Let me be straight. The Framework for Freedom may or may not be as easy as it sounds. Your conscious mind might get on board with your efforts, and you may nod your head as you read along and do the work. But your subconscious mind may try to fight you. It's okay and totally normal to feel that way. I want to remind you that there may be many times in this book when you feel uncomfortable. You are under no obligation to accept everything or anything I'm sharing. After all, one of our primary goals together is to help you get so rock-solid in your own identity and beliefs that you're not unwillingly influenced in any way, shape, or form. Take what you need. Implement as much as you can and choose to do. Stay committed to the process. You're here for a reason. I invite you to take a stand for yourself. Put yourself on the front lines for the sake of your truth. Your breakthrough awaits, but it requires your dedication. We'll keep working at it together. I'm with you.

And remember to stick to the facts. If you must tell stories, tell the stories that serve you best.

Are you ready to tell a new story? Proverbs 18:21 says, "The tongue has the power of life and death" (NIV), and science has proven the benefits of speaking out affirming statements.* If science *and* the spiritual realm can agree on the benefits of speaking affirmations out loud, I

---

* Claude M. Steele, "The Psychology of Self-Affirmation: Sustaining the Integrity of the Self," *Advances in Experimental Social Psychology*, 21, no. 2 (1988): 261–302, https://baltimorewisdomproject.org/uploads/7/0/8/0/70800857/the_psychology_of_self-affirmation.pdf.

think it's safe to say it's worth a try. So before we move forward, I invite you to say this out loud:

——— AFFIRMATION ———

I AM A FACT FINDER AND TRUTH TELLER.

——————————————————— #PermissiontoOffend ———

If you're anything like me, you might feel weird or silly saying an affirmation out loud. That's okay. The more you practice and actually *believe* the statement, the more natural it will become.

PRINCIPLES OF ACTIVATING YOUR TRUTH

▶ The story itself is neutral. A story is neither good nor bad. It's the *meaning* we assign to our stories that drives the emotions and labels of "good" and "bad."
▶ Most of your thoughts happen automatically.
▶ Stories can be conscious or subconscious.
▶ We tell stories that support our beliefs.
▶ You can choose to accept or reject a story at any moment.
▶ Pay attention to the feelings that seemingly pop up out of nowhere. Those are clues that stories are being replayed beneath the surface.
▶ Identifying the facts, separating your stories, questioning those stories, and choosing new beliefs all create an opportunity for healing, intimacy, and freedom in your relationships and your life as a whole.

Now that you've got the Framework for Freedom, practice spending just a few moments each day—whether it's with a journal and pen in hand, or just a mental review—taking inventory, identifying the facts, and separating the stories you've created from your daily experience. Doing this will help you release what has held you back from speaking your truth and getting more of what you want.

You want to enter a market that everyone says is saturated? *You can do that.*

You want to adopt a child as a single woman? *You can do that.*

You want to quit your job and start an entirely new career even though you're over forty? *You can do that.*

Keep reading. You'll get to enjoy real-life stories of women who did all that and more, all because they identified the facts, stopped telling stories that held them down, and started telling stories that allowed them to rise to new heights.

2

DEFINE YOUR
BELIEFS + VALUES

What the heck? This ain't right. These were my thoughts as chunks of hair covered my hairbrush. With each stroke, hundreds of strands gathered on the bristles. I was used to losing a few dozen strands here and there, like any other person. But this wasn't just a few dozen. There were *hundreds*, if not thousands, of hairs clumped together. I laid the brush on my bathroom counter and grabbed the phone.

"Dr. Matt, something's not right. I'm losing a ton of hair. Like for real, for real, chunks! What's happening?"

Two months prior, I had been diagnosed with triple-negative breast cancer, the most aggressive type. The surgery to remove the rapidly growing tumor had been a success, but I wasn't out of the woods yet. According to my oncology team at Baptist MD Anderson Cancer Center in Jacksonville, Florida, I would need aggressive chemotherapy and radiation—almost an entire year's worth of treatments—if I wanted to beat the odds. One of the scariest decisions I've ever had to make in my life was to go against the advice of those trained medical professionals.

I politely but firmly declined their treatment plan and set out

on my own healing journey. I'll never forget the look of disgust—
yes, disgust—given to me by my chemotherapy oncologist. Her face
scrunched up as if some foul odor had taken over the room. And I
sensed she felt a combination of pity and disbelief as I rejected her
plan. Now I'm 100 percent certain I was telling stories in my head
about her facial expressions and what she might have been thinking,
so let me give you the facts.

I don't know what your experience has been concerning your
health, but the part I haven't yet told you is that I had already been
dismissed by two other doctors before getting diagnosed.

The first doctor told me it was just a complex cyst and I had
nothing to worry about. "A complex cyst? What does that mean?
Are there simple cysts?" I asked, thinking I was being funny. "Yes,
actually there are," she replied. "A simple cyst is fluid filled, and
complex cysts usually have some debris. Follow up with your primary, but you should be fine." And that was it. She was out the
door.

Listen, that wasn't gonna cut it for me. There was a lump and I
needed a more definitive answer other than "you should be fine."
"Should be" and "will be" are not the same.

The next doctor I saw told me, "You're young. You have no history of breast cancer. Let's wait and see. We'll have you come back
in three months." *Wait and see? Are you crazy?* I thought and then
said out loud, "Sir, you're crazy if you think I'm leaving here without
an appointment for a mammogram and some kind of diagnostic for
what this thing is." I was half joking by calling him crazy but full serious about wanting answers. And *thank God!* I didn't leave that office
when that man told me to wait and see because within three weeks of
being diagnosed, the tumor had advanced from stage 1 to stage 2b.

If I had waited three months to "see," I have no doubt in my mind
that I would have been stage 3 for sure and probably stage 4. It was
my willingness to remove the filter—the shame of questioning and

the fear of overstepping—that allowed me to give myself permission to offend and advocate for myself.

So now you understand why I was telling myself stories when the chemotherapy oncologist was rolling her eyes and scrunching her face at me, right? I had already been snubbed on repeat by these medical experts. I was done with other people telling me what was right for *me*.

Permission Slip

I give myself permission to advocate for myself and trust in my decisions.

#PermissiontoOffend

To be fair, my other two oncologists (surgical and radiation) were more compassionate and even somewhat supportive, but I could see the fear and sadness in their eyes as I said, "No, thank you." They didn't believe my plan was the best option, but I had to trust myself. It wasn't a coincidence that a friend, knowing how much I love documentaries, had sent me one on naturopathic modalities for healing cancer just a few months prior to my diagnosis. It wasn't a coincidence that I met a woman who knew of a research hospital outside the country that was using the very same therapies I had seen in that documentary. It wasn't a coincidence that I had a sudden massive cash injection in my bank account that allowed me to pay for most of the treatments that weren't covered by our standard insurance. (P.S. I'll tell you all about how I got that massive cash injection in chapter 9.)

Take note:
Stop mistaking God's divine guidance for random coincidence.

STOP MISTAKING GOD'S DIVINE GUIDANCE FOR RANDOM COINCIDENCE.

I had to trust God and myself—*even if it meant offending the entire medical community in Jacksonville!* This was my *life* we were talking about. I didn't have time to argue or prove anything to them or anyone else. I needed to trust what I knew in my heart to be the right move for me. Do you know what it's like to feel that level of conviction? Have you ever experienced what seem to be coincidences but deep down you know are winks from God? Take a moment to remember that it's safe to trust yourself.

Except in this particular moment, staring at my scalp in the mirror as I waited for Dr. Matt to give me a logical explanation, I suddenly wasn't feeling so confident in my decision to skip out on Baptist MD Anderson and their standard-of-care treatment plan. Maybe I had made a mistake after all.

Dr. Matt was one of my doctors from the cancer research hospital in Mexico where I underwent treatment. I spent three weeks receiving a wide variety of alternative treatments that aren't standard of care in the United States. Dr. Matt assured me the hair loss was probably just a combination of stress and my recent weight loss. During my stay there, I had lost over twenty-five pounds. Standing only four feet, eleven and a half inches, I now weighed a whopping ninety-nine pounds. According to Dr. Matt, the hair loss was probably just my body's response to the sudden drop in body mass.

"Try and relax, Rachel. Keep eating, keep juicing, *rest*. I'm sure you're trying to go back to full speed, but you need to give yourself time to rest." *I swear if these doctors tell me to rest one more time* . . . "You can't be the hard charger right now." Dr. Matt gave me clear orders to slow down, eat, and rest. I felt optimistic about my hair but frustrated with his instructions.

"You can't be the hard charger right now." His words echoed in my head. *But I am a hard charger. I'm a former US Marine. Hard charging is what I do. It's who I am.* I was on the borderline of falling into the identity trap, but I caught myself. *No, Rachel. That's not who you are. That's what you did. Don't confuse your roles and responsibilities with who you are.*

I had given that same bit of advice to others many times over, and now here I was, having to swallow my own pills. It's easy to confuse our identity with the roles and responsibilities that we assign to ourselves or that have been assigned to us by others. Go to any networking event, social gathering, or interview and you're likely to hear a conversation like this: "Tell me about yourself." "Well, I'm a mom, a coach, a . . ."—insert the role or responsibility. Say it out loud regularly and it becomes part of your programming. Stay in the role long enough and it practically becomes part of your DNA. There's nothing wrong with loving those roles, but ultimately, you are not the role or responsibility you've taken on or been assigned.

DON'T CONFUSE YOUR ROLES AND RESPONSIBILITIES WITH WHO YOU ARE.

#PermissiontoOffend

Armed with my own self-talk and Dr. Matt's encouragement, I did my best to relax. I scheduled massages, I listened to guided prayers, I watched my favorite shows and read encouraging books. But three weeks later the situation went from bad to worse. I was waking up to find thousands of hair strands on my pillowcase, large chunks of hair falling out in my hands as I washed my hair, and finally, a piercing bald spot. *This. Is. Not. Right! I didn't even do real chemo. What's happening to me?*

Frantically, I left messages for my after-care team in Mexico and called Dr. Matt. "Dr. Matt! What. Is. Going. On!?" I asked, trying not to go all the way off on him, but also not masking my anger or fear.

"Well, sweetheart, I've only ever seen this three times in all the years I've been here, but very rarely, some patients lose their hair because of the IPT."

What?! Lose my hair? This wasn't the deal. Hysterical thoughts raced through my mind.

The IPT Dr. Matt was referring to is insulin potentiation therapy, a somewhat "experimental" (depending on who you ask) form of low-dose chemotherapy that mixes insulin with a reduced dose of conventional chemotherapy. Most people who go through IPT do not experience any of the standard discomforts of conventional chemotherapy, like nausea, vomiting, or hair loss. In fact, hair loss is so rare it wasn't even mentioned to me as a possibility.

"In almost five years and thousands of patients we've treated, you're the fourth person I've ever seen this happen to," Dr. Matt continued.

Is he for real? With my standard defense sarcasm, I replied, "Well, it's only fitting that my exceptional self would be the exception this time. So, what does this mean? Am I going to lose all my hair?" I asked, half expecting him to say no—that this was just a fluke.

"Probably," he said bluntly.

So there it was. I was going to lose my hair after all. *Sigh.*

WHO AM I?

The time had come. My hair had been falling out at such a rapid pace that I had started wearing hats and scarves all day, every day. I avoided the mirror because it was so jarring to see my reflection. For the first time in the entire cancer journey, *I looked sick.* I didn't recognize myself, and each day was becoming harder than the day before. So I did it. I set a date and time to shave my head, live, on social media.

I flipped open my laptop, set my chair to face the screen, turned up some praise music, and reached for the clippers. Taking a deep breath, I said, "I believe God can use our most heartbreaking moment to give us our most powerful breakthrough . . . And I thought about wearing makeup today because I don't know what I'll look like without hair. But God loves me with or without hair or makeup, and I want to take this opportunity to love me, with or without hair, without makeup, just as I am . . ." I began to choke up as tears rolled down my cheeks. As bravely as I could, I began to buzz through my almost nonexistent locks of hair. The whole thing took only a few minutes, with my husband and daughters each taking a turn shearing off the last remnants of my hair. When it was over, I felt empowered. And to my surprise, I was really feeling myself. *Okay, bald head! Go on with your bad self, Rachel. You look cute. You can pull it off.* I affirmed myself. Family and friends affirmed me as well. But what no one told me was that shaving your head doesn't stop your hair from falling out. It just helps you look slightly more presentable in the short-term.

While shaving my head had been empowering, what followed turned out to be traumatizing. My hair continued to fall out, but this time, rather than clumps of long strands, thousands of short clippings were being left behind. My hair now looked patchy and uneven. Everywhere I went, I could see people looking at me with a question mark in their eyes. At first I thought it was just in my head, my own insecurities. But my suspicions were confirmed one sunny afternoon as I pulled up to the guard shack of my neighborhood to pick up my mail. Ron, our day-shift guard, looked at me, slightly hesitant, with his head cocked to one side. I knew what he wanted to ask. I could see it in his eyes. He just didn't know how to get the words out, so I threw him a bone. "Yes," I said. I didn't need to say anything else.

A look of relief swept over his face and he said, "My wife went through it too and she's just fine! Matter of fact, she's at home right now. You're going to be fine too, Ms. Luna."

"I know I am, Ron." I said, trying to reassure myself as much as he was reassuring me. He raised the gate arm for me, and as I drove up the road to my home, I sighed. This was my new normal: strange looks, questioning glances, spectator eyes filled with what I presumed to be pity.

I had never realized how much of my identity as a woman was tied to my hair. Added to the fact that by choosing to try to heal naturally, I had taken on an entirely new clean way of life and, wearing makeup, which is, sadly, full of chemicals, was out of the question. False eyelashes? Also not approved. Everything I did was an effort to detoxify my body, which meant avoiding the conventional, highly encouraged practices like manicures and pedicures, which are often touted as "self-care." In my case, to indulge in those chemical-filled and often toxic experiences would have been self-harm. No shade to you if you have a standing mani-pedi appointment and a routine six-week root touch-up. Live your life. But for me, this new lifestyle—this attempt to radically improve my odds of living beyond the five-year survival rate—was challenging everything about who I thought I was and the life I had set out to live. In this particular moment, I was forced to answer questions I had never once considered:

Who am I without my hair?

Who am I without makeup and lashes?

Who am I when all the things that help me identify as a woman are stripped away?

As I answered those questions I realized that, at first, I was someone who avoided mirrors and photos. Which is why, regrettably, I don't have many photos of myself during that season.

There will most certainly come a moment when you too will have crossed the valley and want a reminder of how far you've come.

NOTE TO SELF

DOCUMENT THE DIFFICULT.

#PermissiontoOffend

Then, I was someone who made her best attempt to walk her talk. I began forcing myself to look in the mirror and recognize beauty beyond societal conventions. I repeatedly told myself, "I love you just the way you are." It felt odd at first. Almost fake. But soon I began to believe the words coming out of my mouth. I now know telling myself, "I love you just the way you are," was difficult and felt fake because deep down I didn't mean it, nor did I believe anyone could or would love me as I was. Despite having a loving family, clients, students, and even strangers on the internet who messaged me, saying they loved me, I was always waiting for them to turn around and reject me. This new image of myself forced me to deal with my underlying childhood trauma and stories of rejection, things I thought I had dealt with but were obviously still lingering. It was doing the work you did in chapter 1—*Every. Single. Day.*—that helped me create a new belief pattern for myself.

Then one day I *meant* those words. For the first time in my life, I could see who I was at my soul level. The words poured out of my mouth:

I am God's masterpiece.

I am loving.

I am lovable.

I. AM. LOVE.

And just like that, my hair grew back. Okay, maybe not *just like that*, but I promise you, something shifted, and as soon as I accepted myself without any additives, it seemed as though my hair grew back at warp speed. Not only that, it grew back thicker, fuller, and curly, just like I had asked God and prayed for. Interesting how once we surrender, *(almost)* everything we want becomes available to us.

So I learned that my identity is rooted in *love*.

IDENTITY CRISIS INTERVENTION

"Yes, I feel certain in who I am 99 percent of the time," my friend Andrea said with total confidence when I asked if she felt rooted in her identity. *Of course she did!* Andrea is one of those women who just *knows*. You know what I mean? She knows what she wants, goes straight after it, rarely ever hesitates, and has full confidence that everything will work out in her favor. Me, on the other hand, not so much. My automatic mental response at that time was: *I don't.* It was true. I thought, *Most days I'm not sure of who I am.* As more thoughts began to swirl through my consciousness, I felt a lump welling in my throat. Not a painful, gut-wrenching lump but the kind you might get when you feel like you're about to cry.

Feeling great sorrow and great joy simultaneously is a really interesting experience. Rather than fight it, I decided to lean in and embrace them both. Positive thoughts danced in my head. *How lucky am I? Every day that I don't feel rooted is a chance for me to choose who I am. When my identity is in question, I get to choose who I want to be. I get to experiment and play.* I felt a pep in my step as I celebrated and embraced a part of myself I had previously chastised. I used to think something was wrong with me because I was so uncertain of my identity, but reframing this thought gave me a sense of relief. *I get to choose who I want to be every day.*

Permission Slip

I give myself permission to add more fun, joy, and play into my life.

#PermissiontoOffend

Imagine if we allowed ourselves the opportunity to "play" more in life. Imagine if *you* allowed yourself more play. What if instead of trying to fit into the constraints of so-called societal norms, you played around with who you want to be and the impact you want to have on this world? This is where having a clear picture of your beliefs and values helps you define your identity.

For example, wandering around in this state of uncertainty is actually an opportunity for me, as a Christian woman, to connect with God on a daily basis. Why? Because I believe in God. I believe what God's word says about me (lots of wonderful things about who I am and the image in which I was created). I value my faith. I value having an intimate relationship with the entity I believe created the universe. I also find it a bit comical that much of this process is devoted to choosing my own thoughts, beliefs, and values, and yet one of my strategies to help me decide on them is to go back to God so I can be reminded of who He says I am. Basically, I'm allowing the principles of the Bible to become my imposed beliefs. Dare I say it? I'm allowing God's values to become imposed on me. That makes me chuckle. But hey, it's a choice at the end of the day. I get to validate or disprove what God says. I am still in control of my freewill choices. And you, my friend, are also still in control. No matter what you subscribe to, no matter what your dogma is or isn't, the reality is that on any given day, you get to choose who you want to be based on what you believe and value.

By the way, I'm pleased to announce that, like my friend Andrea, I'm now certain of who I am 99 percent of the time. On days when I'm teetering in the 1 percent identity crisis, I go through all the steps I'm about to outline for you and I give myself permission to play. I'm excited for you to do the same!

YOU'RE INVITED BY DEFAULT

Leading up to her fortieth birthday, my friend Patrice Washington wrote on social media, "Do you ever wonder who you could become if you dropped some of the labels you've allowed to be assigned to you? I'm turning 40 soon and I'm feeling led to unpack, unlearn and question EVERYTHING just to make sure who I am in this next phase of my life is what I choose and not what was chosen for me. You're invited by default."*

---

* Patrice C. Washington (@SeekWisdomPCW), "Do you ever wonder . . ." Instagram, February 17, 2021, https://www.instagram.com/p/CLaZpbzJrOV/?hl=en.

First of all, can we talk about how good that post was? I mean, come through with the wisdom, friend! I wasn't the only one who felt that way. Comments flooded the thread. Literally hundreds of women shared the labels, roles, and identities that had been imposed upon them:

I'm tired of being the one who has her life together.

I'm the "irresponsible one" in the family simply because I choose to live a nomadic lifestyle.

I've held on to guilt for not being as responsible as others expect.

I'm not allowed to fall apart because I'm the mom.

Show no weakness. Do not cry. Do not ask for help.

The comments on Patrice's post were powerful reminders for me to question everything I believe, and question it *often*.

Permission Slip

I give myself permission to question, unpack, and unlearn everything I believe.

#PermissiontoOffend

What about you? Are you ready to question some things? Is there any label you're ready to rethink? Who are you when you remove the labels, roles, and responsibilities? Moreover, how has holding on to them kept you from speaking up, taking action on your desires, and doing more of what you want? Let's find out together so you can start walking in your truth.

DEFINING IDENTITY

First, let's agree that, for the purpose of our work together, we're going to define identity as the sum of our beliefs plus our values. For the record, identity in this context is centered around personal identity, not the "Big 8" socially constructed identities (race, ethnicity, sexual orientation, gender identity, ability, religion/spirituality, nationality, and socioeconomics).* Today you're working on your *personal* identity and you'll be defining it using a simple formula:

| BELIEFS + VALUES = IDENTITY |

BELIEFS: an acceptance that a statement is true or that something exists; trust, faith, or confidence in someone or something.

VALUES: a person's principles or standards of behavior; one's judgment of what is important in life.

Our beliefs amplify our identity, and as mentioned in chapter 1, some of your beliefs may have been imposed on you by caregivers, teachers, or leaders. This is why so many people struggle with identity. They have been living their lives based on someone else's belief and value system. One comment I've heard from others is "At my age . . ." followed by a limiting belief. Understand this: you get to redefine your identity every day, at any age. There is no "top of

---

* Admin, "FAQ: What Are Cultural Identifiers," *Library and Information Science Network* (blog), December 2, 2021, https://www.ywboston.org/2020/10/your-full-self-social-identities-and-the-workplace/.

the mountain." Life is a journey and death is the final stop. As long as you have breath, you have a chance.

To begin defining your identity, you'll first have to examine your beliefs:

What do you believe to be true about you?

Who do you believe you are?

What do you believe is available for you?

What do you believe you are worthy of having?

Most people will read these questions and gloss right over them. I believe a few people might pause for a second or two to consider each question, but then they too, without actually answering the questions, will move on. A very, very, very small percentage of people will take the time to grab a journal or a piece of paper and write the answers down. Be part of the small percentage. Like my friend Elizabeth Benton Thompson says, "Don't confuse information and implementation."*

I'll add to that: Don't just stop at implementation; strive for integration. To integrate means to embrace and take on these practices as part of your consistent flow.

Another practical way you can examine your beliefs if you don't feel ready or particularly interested in answering the previous questions (yet) is to take a look at the results in your life. Your results are a reflection of your beliefs. For example, if you say you believe that you are ready to make a change in your life but you lack faith to take action, then it's an indication that some part of you doesn't actually believe you'll be supported in the actions you take.

---

* Elizabeth Benton Thompson, *Tools for the Trenches: Daily Practices for Resilience, Perspective & Progress* (Primal Potential, 2022), 14.

ALIGNMENT OPPORTUNITY

What's one result you've created in the last twelve months? Identify the actions you took (or didn't take), the feelings you experienced, and the belief(s) you held leading up to, during, and after the result.

One result I've created in the last twelve months is:

The actions (or inactions) I took to achieve that result were:

Before taking/not taking action, I felt:

Before taking/not taking action, I thought:

After taking/not taking action, I believed:

Reflecting on this result, what do/did I believe about myself?

This alignment opportunity might get a little scary, especially if you identify a negative result that ties back to a negative belief you have about yourself. Not to worry—help is on the way in chapter 3. You keep going. It's going to be so worth it! Affirm yourself in this work right now.

PRINCIPLES OF DEFINING YOUR BELIEFS

▶ Confusing your roles and responsibilities with your identity is detrimental to your truth.

▶ Document the difficult, even if you don't feel like it in the moment. It will serve you and potentially others in the future.

▶ Beliefs + Values = Identity. Your beliefs and your values amplify your identity, so make sure to examine them often.

▶ Question *everything* just to make sure who you are is who you have chosen to be and not what was chosen for you.

──────── **AFFIRMATION** ────────

I GET TO CHOOSE MY BELIEFS, MY VALUES, AND WHO I WANT TO BE EVERY SINGLE DAY.

──────────────────────── #PermissiontoOffend ────────

Are you starting to pick up on the pattern I've laced throughout this book? Giving yourself permission to offend is a by-product of asking and answering meaningful questions. By answering the questions and taking advantage of this chapter's alignment opportunity, you've taken the first step in defining your identity.

I am so curious to know what you discovered, or rediscovered, about yourself. Sometimes we forget who we are and what we believe because we're so inundated with information. But isn't it nice to take a step back and reflect on what's true for you? If you feel led to share, go ahead and send me an email at hello@rachelluna.biz and tell me as much or as little as you want. Bonus points if you take a picture of any of your alignment opportunities completed. I might even send you a little thank-you gift for reaching out! No pressure, though. You do you, boo.

Meet me in the next chapter, where we'll go one layer deeper on beliefs and then I'll walk you through a revelatory values alignment opportunity that is so good, my clients and students are always wide-eyed after completing it.

See you there!

3
ANCHOR YOUR IDENTITY

He kept me for about six months after my mother died, but the grief of losing the love of his life, his struggles with substance abuse, and the question of his own mortality—he too was HIV positive at the time—made my father less than capable of caring for a little girl. Shortly after my fourth birthday, he dropped me off at my godmother's house and left me there for good.

My new home, built in 1901, was a three-story, ten-room, legal two-family house in East New York, Brooklyn. If you walked through the wooden double-door entrance, you would encounter a narrow foyer with a staircase to the right, a wall with two doors on the left, and a bathroom at the end, opposite the front door. It always struck me as an awkward entryway. Why was the bathroom in the hallway? If the bathroom door was left open, you could see visitors coming and going. It was in this bathroom that I experienced my first heartbreak.

I don't remember anything else about that particular day other than sitting in the bathtub, crying out to my father as he walked out the front door. "Daddy, please don't leave me. Daddy, please don't go. Daddy!" My entire body shook as I sat, sobbing under the hot water, my little arms hugging my legs. I didn't understand what I had done wrong or why he was leaving. He was there one minute, telling me he loved me, and the next moment, just like that, he was gone.

My godmother, the only true mother I have ever known, and whom I have always referred to as my mom (and will do so throughout this book), became my legal guardian. Although she was and continues to be the most amazing mother I could have ever asked for, her presence never made up for the pain and abandonment I felt from being left behind by my father.

To be fair, it's not as if I never saw my father again. He was intermittently present in my life. My mom was the driving force behind keeping my relationship with my father alive. It was her constant encouragement for me to call him that kept us connected. Left up to my father, I'd be lucky to get a call on the holidays or several days past my birthday. But when we spoke, he praised me endlessly. He told me how much he loved me, how much he missed me, and how proud of me he was. Our calls never ended without a "Three, two, one, hit it!" countdown to hang up. And while there were numerous times when he made plans to come and pick me up for a weekend, only to leave me waiting with my bags packed, when we did have our sporadic visits, he went out of his way to shower me with kisses, words of affirmation, and constant praise.

When we were together, my dad made me feel like the most important person on the planet. He repeatedly told me, "Education first, boys second," impressing upon me the importance of having an education to fall back on, but always encouraging me to have and pursue my dreams. He made me feel unstoppable when we were together. But then the visit would come to an end, and days would turn into months before I heard from him again.

That night in the bathtub, I told myself, "I'm not good enough." Because he didn't take me with him, I decided I wasn't worthy. Along with that story, I told myself, unconsciously at the time, "Everyone I love leaves me." I began to collect evidence of these stories I told myself, and several years later, when my father got married for the first and only time, never having married my biological mother, those stories became more solidified. When he married, not only did he take on the responsibility of supporting his wife but he also took on the responsibility of raising her daughter. Mind you, whenever I would call and ask my dad to pick me up for a weekend he would often say he couldn't because he didn't have money. Seemed to me like he had plenty of money for his new wife and her daughter.

I wondered, *Why is he raising her and not me? I'm the one who doesn't have a mother.* It was yet another story I told myself, because the fact was (and is), I have an amazing, phenomenal, loving mother—my godmother, who treated me like her own biological daughter. However, at ten or eleven, in my mind, I was "the girl who didn't have a mom." My dad was raising a girl who had a mom, and it wasn't fair. With my limited life experience, I decided it meant there was something wrong with me. I wasn't good enough. Otherwise, he would have kept me. If I was special and worthy, he'd find a way to include me in his new family. But that never happened.

Those stories played on repeat in my mind, and I carried them with me through the years, constantly looking for evidence to prove them true. This constant need to be "right" in my stories led me to choose the wrong men over and over again. I chose men I knew, going into the relationship, were not good for me. Players, guys who were not ready for relationships, and even guys who were verbally, emotionally, and one time physically abusive. When they left, when we broke up, or when they cheated on me, as many did, I went right back to my story: *I'm not good enough.* If I were good enough, they wouldn't treat me that way. If I were good enough, they would cherish, appreciate, and care for me.

These experiences also supported the story I told myself on a subconscious level: *Men I love always leave me.* Because, after all, my own father had left. My father, the man who was supposed to love me and take care of me and be my hero, had left, so of course any other man was bound to leave. If my own dad didn't stick around, why would some stranger?

Those were just a few of the stories I told myself growing up. The more I replayed the stories, the more I believed them. Each one chipped away at my confidence, later in life sending me into a downward spiral of depression, disordered eating, promiscuity, and alcohol addiction.

IMPACT ON IDENTITY

It has been said that belief is the foundation of joy and peace. But what happens when your foundation starts off fractured or, through some sort of life quake, becomes unstable? In my case, these stories produced beliefs that created conflict in my identity. My personal identity was so influenced by these negative beliefs that they deeply affected how I saw myself and what I believed I was worthy to be, do, and have.

Remember the alignment opportunity in chapter 2 (page 60)? If I were to use one of my old toxic romantic relationships as the result in that activity, then it's easy to trace back to the actions, feelings, and ultimately my belief that I wasn't worthy of having a loving, supportive man in my life. See how stories influence our beliefs, create our results, and ultimately affect our identity?

I wonder what stories and beliefs have affected your identity. Have they been positive, negative, or maybe a combination? Moreover, which beliefs have you committed to that might need to be released?

RELEASING BELIEFS AND OLD SHAME

For years I was committed to my "belief" (which we both now know was a story) that my dad abandoned me. I didn't know or realize it then, but holding on to that story was what created many of my limiting beliefs. This is why it is so important that you start with the alignment opportunity exercises in chapter 1. Even if you've done them before, I have found that, like working out, cleanses and detoxes, this work is best repeated often to ensure your mind is as strong as your body.

As I previously mentioned, my dominant limiting belief has always been *I'm not good enough*. Granted, I don't recall spending days agonizing and thinking that I wasn't good enough. Nope, my thoughts were way more cunning and deceptive than to just hang out on Front Street like that. Rather, my *I'm not good enough* sounded more like *These graphics won't resonate with anyone* or *I have nothing interesting to share* or *Who's gonna want this offer? No one! Besides, a hundred other people are already doing that.*

Instead of fighting *I'm not good enough* head-on, I often don't realize I'm feeling that way until I've already been hit where it hurts—in my relationships, in my work, and through my family.

When I was single and hoeing around—yes, I said hoeing—for a long time I felt a sense of shame about how I bounced from boy to boy, looking for love, attention, and acceptance. But I've learned a few things about shame over the years.

1. Shame is not who you are. Shame is the feeling produced from taking (or not taking) actions that don't align with your true identity. I am not shameful for sleeping with boys, but it was a shame that I felt I needed to sleep with them to find love and attention.

2. No one can shame you. *No one.* In the last decade or so a term has emerged that, in my opinion, has been really detrimental and disempowering to us as a society but, in particular, marginalized communities. It's this notion of "being shamed." Countless articles have been written about fat-shaming, mom-shaming, slut-shaming, skinny-shaming. Pick a noun and add the word "shame" and there you go. But NO ONE CAN SHAME YOU UNLESS YOU LET THEM!!

I'm not sorry I'm screaming. Be offended if I've triggered you. We are the change makers and leaders of this world. You and I have the power to effect change in our homes, communities, businesses, and beyond. So let's have tough conversations and do the things that will actually help others find freedom.

Permission Slip

I give myself permission to release any shame I've held on to or allowed others to project on me.

#PermissiontoOffend

Here's the point that I'm inviting you to explore concerning shame and shaming: you are in more control than you've accepted.

When you fall into the trap of believing that someone is "shaming" you, you are giving them your power. It doesn't have to be that way. You don't have to live as a victim even after being victimized. Take ownership of everything and every moment that has helped you become who you are. *That* is how you stop letting others shame you. *That* is how you start giving yourself permission to offend!

When I think back on those days when I was behaving promiscuously, I believe I was a sad girl who was desperate for her father's love, attention, and acceptance. And when I didn't get it, I tried to fill the gap with anyone who looked my way. I was hurt and hurting but didn't have the knowledge or communication skills to ask for help.

Next time you feel someone has shamed you, ask yourself, *Would I let a child believe she was shameful for doing the same thing?* I hope I've made the argument for you to treat yourself the same way. Beyond the argument to treat yourself more kindly, I hope you'll remember that while you may have done some shameful things in the past, you are not the shame of those acts. As long as you can release the negative belief, you can release the shame!

GETTING ROOTED

It's time to identify the limiting beliefs that aren't serving you. Remember how we discussed the fact that most thoughts happen automatically? Well, that's exactly what a limiting belief is.* It's an automatic thought that tends to pop into your head and stops you whenever you try to do something outside your comfort zone. These thoughts often occur when you try to do something that will effect a positive change in your life. If you've ever had a dream or

---

* Jane, "What Are Your Biggest Limiting Beliefs?," Habits for WellBeing, March 2020, https://www.habitsforwellbeing.com/what-are-your-biggest-limiting-beliefs/.

big desire that just never seemed to manifest into reality, it's likely that what has stood in your way is one or more limiting beliefs. But don't be deceived; not all limiting beliefs are bad. Like our stories, some of these limiting beliefs actually serve us. For example, holding the belief that mouthing off to a parent is wrong saved me from getting multiple *chancletazos*—otherwise known as a smack to the head with a house slipper that has been flung across the room at superhuman speed by a Puerto Rican mother whose accuracy could rival that of a Patriot missile. Keeping my mouth shut when I really wanted to tell her about herself was the work of a limiting belief serving me well.

> LIMITING BELIEF: A LIMITING BELIEF IS A STATE OF MIND, CONVICTION, OR BELIEF YOU THINK TO BE TRUE THAT LIMITS YOU IN SOME WAY.
>
> #PermissiontoOffend

On the other hand, *I'm not good enough*—the limiting belief that has been most prominent in my life—has stopped me from going after a plethora of opportunities and delayed the manifestation of many of my God-given dreams. The irony is that I have never consciously thought, *I'm not good enough,* even at times when that would have been a very appropriate thought. Rather, in most cases, my conscious thoughts were more along the lines of: *Yeah, that's a good idea. I'll add that to the list and do it later.*

Limiting beliefs are often tricky little deceivers that manifest in disguise. *I'm not good enough* might show up in your mind as a voice that says, *I'm not smart. I can't do it because* _____

_____ [insert whatever reason you believe you

can't do something]. *So-and-so is better than me. So-and-so already did it. I'm lazy.*

Here are some other examples of limiting beliefs that can hide in plain sight:

The world isn't a safe place.

I don't know enough.

I'm not qualified.

I feel unworthy.

I don't have time.

I don't have the energy.

Any of these sound familiar? Maybe yes, maybe no, so let's keep going.

UNCOVERING BELIEFS, BECAUSE...

You may be thinking, *I don't know my limiting belief.* Or your ego might be trying to tell you that you don't have any limiting beliefs. Girl, bye. Admitting there's a problem is the first step to the solution. Make no mistake: allowing your non-serving limiting beliefs to hide in the background is a big problem, and it's what's been holding you back all this time—holding you back from speaking your mind, from applying for a promotion, from changing careers, from starting your business, from whatever it is that you don't yet have but deeply desire. These beliefs may not be persistent. They may come and go depending on the situation, but you've got at least one. Let's find it now, because when we do, you'll be that much closer to a breakthrough.

Here we go. Answer these questions. (Yes, more questions because the more questions you answer, the closer you'll get to your truth, and you already know—*the truth shall set you free!*)

What's one thing you want to be, do, or have that hasn't manifested in your life yet?

Why not?

What limiting belief(s) can you identify?

If you're having trouble figuring out your limiting beliefs, try this simple method, which I learned from therapist Andy Hunt. All you have to do is complete the following sentence:

I can't _____

because _____.

Example: I can't achieve my dreams because I'm too old.

Let's try that again.

I can't _____

because _____.

The power of this exercise is in the word "because." What follows "because" is a reason. And hiding beneath the reason is a belief.

But remember, limiting beliefs are often subconscious. The example "I can't achieve my dreams because I'm too old" is from my client Sandy, who recently turned forty years old. When I asked her if she believed women her age were too old to achieve their dreams, she said no. But when she thought of herself, she believed *she* was too old. That was her limiting belief.

───── ENCOURAGEMENT ─────

IF YOU FIND YOURSELF THINKING *I DON'T KNOW* IN RESPONSE TO ANY OF THE QUESTIONS, JUST WRITE WHATEVER COMES TO MIND. OFTEN, "I DON'T KNOW" IS A FILLER STATEMENT WE USE WHEN WE HAVEN'T TAKEN THE TIME TO THINK ABOUT OUR ANSWER OR WHEN WE'RE SCARED TO ADMIT OUR TRUTH. IT'S OKAY. DO YOUR BEST. WRITE ANYTHING TO START.

──────────────── #PermissiontoOffend ────

Let's go back through the questions together.

Choose a problem or desire in your life right now. Try not to judge yourself. We've all got problems, and we for sure all have desires. Even the person who always looks put together has her own personal problem that keeps her up at night and something on her vision board she can't stop thinking about. She's just using a really good filter to hide her insecurities and fears. Don't believe the hype. Just pick the problem or desire that feels most pressing right now, and write it as a simple statement:

My most pressing problem or desire right now is _____

_____.

Next, fill in the blanks with why you think you have not been able to remedy this problem or have not manifested what you desire in your life.

I can't _____

because _____ .

After the "because," list all the reasons (use the following blank lines or a separate sheet of paper if needed). For example, a reason you can't lose weight might be:

I can't lose weight because I don't have time to cook.

A reason why you haven't asked for a raise might be:

I can't ask for a raise because they'll think I'm greedy or ungrateful.

List all the reasons here (or in your journal):

_____

_____

_____

_____

Once you've made your list of reasons, say them out loud. You may feel silly, but I know from experience that when we hear our thoughts out loud, they sound vastly different from how they play in our minds. Say them out loud right now.

Did you say them out loud? Okay, next. Write down whatever comes into your head. Do this quickly and without judgment, until you run out of thoughts or you find yourself repeating the same reasons. In the previous example about weight loss, the thought behind the reason might be:

I don't have time to cook because everyone needs my help in the evenings, and if I don't help, homework and chores won't get done, and I'll be a bad mom and wife.

You see how quickly all that spiraled from a desire to lose weight to suddenly being a bad mom? Geez! And we do this all the time without even realizing it's happening.

The final step to uncover your limiting beliefs is to look at your list of thoughts, read each statement out loud, and evaluate how much of it is fact and how much of it is story.

To determine your current dominant limiting belief, look for the false belief that is showing up most frequently. Remember, you may not (and most likely don't) have just one limiting belief. Don't be alarmed if you have several. But there should be one that feels like it plays more of a role in your emotional life. For instance, if the belief "I can't lose weight because I don't feel worthy of love" feels super significant, that's the one you want to focus on clearing first.

───── ENCOURAGEMENT ─────────────

WHILE WRITING THIS BOOK, I DID EVERY SINGLE ONE OF THE EXERCISES MYSELF (SO I COULD BE IN THE TRENCHES WITH YOU), AND I CAN HONESTLY TELL YOU, SOME OF THEM WERE HARD! REAL TALK: SOME OF THEM STRAIGHT-UP SUCKED BECAUSE THEY FORCED ME TO GO DEEP INTO MY BS. DO YOUR BEST. PUSH PAST THE RESISTANCE. IT'S WORTH IT!

──────────────────────── #PermissiontoOffend ───────

DON'T LET YOUR SITUATION
DEFINE YOUR IDENTITY

"I don't want to take a pill for the rest of my life. I'm not a pill popper! That's not who I am." My friend Keri had just been told she would need major surgery to remove a tumor mass on her adrenal gland. Following the operation, her surgeon told her she'd need to take a pill once a day for the rest of her life to prevent future complications. This bit of news was infuriating to her. As I listened to her rant, I was pretty amused. As someone who downs no less than forty individual pills a day, I, for one, qualify as a so-called pill popper. And I'm not gonna lie: I was also a bit annoyed at what I perceived to be childish behavior on her part. Did she not understand how lucky she was? I would *love* to only need to take *one* pill a day. Judgments began to form, and as I heard them creeping in, I paused and reminded myself how scared she must be.

This is how mastering the Permission to Offend principles helps keep our relationships strong and healthy. Because I've done this work on a daily basis, I'm able to have my judgmental moment—which, as you may recall, is often automatic, not intentional—but rather than sit in that negative space, I move on from it quickly and compassionately. Often judgment isn't rooted in malice; it's rooted in fear. I was judging my friend's response to her journey through my identity as a "pill popper." Recognizing this within just a few moments, I was able to find delight in our convo, and I approached her with genuine care, concern, and love.

I lightly said, "Well, you know I'm president of the Pill Poppers Club and we welcome you," chuckling to try to help ease her fears. Then I said, "But I also think it's interesting that the idea of taking one pill a day for the rest of your life is bringing up so much anger. What does being a pill popper mean to you?" I try hard not to be an unsolicited coach to my friends, but in this case, I just couldn't help myself. My curiosity surrounding her innermost thoughts and the meanings she was assigning to these stories got the better of me.

"It means that everything I've done to stay healthy was for nothing. It means that I'm going to end up just like my family—fat and disease ridden—and I am not like them!"

Permission Slip

I give myself permission to adopt new beliefs that amplify my ability to walk in the identity of someone who already is, does, and has everything they desire.

#PermissiontoOffend

There it was. The root of her anger toward taking a life-saving pill had nothing to do with the pill and everything to do with the identity she never wanted to assume: fat, disease-ridden pill pop-per. In her mind, taking pills meant being unhealthy. I could see how painful and scary this idea was to her. You have to understand, Keri is an organic farmer. Okay, she's not a commercial farmer, but in the backyard of her modest Los Angeles home, Keri grows a variety of organic produce. One of her dreams is to open a farm-to-table restaurant and feed people great quality food. Surely she couldn't be a pill-popping, disease-ridden person and also own a farm-to-table restaurant. The mere suggestion of taking one pill a day was fracturing Keri's entire foundation of who she was.

We continued to work together for a few more minutes, but I could tell my excavation of her deepest thoughts were fueling her fire rather than comforting her. Before we ended our talk, I challenged her: "Why don't you spend some time thinking about what this means to you and where the facts of your stories lie? What new belief can you adopt to help you feel more aligned with your next steps?"

Like Keri, the ball is in your court. Now that you've identified a limiting belief or two, you have the opportunity to move forward and give yourself permission to offend by adopting a new belief—one that amplifies, not limits, your ability to walk in the identity of someone who already is, does, and has everything they desire.

What new or different belief can you align with that will better serve you moving forward? Practice saying this belief out loud on a daily basis. If you really want to embody this work, I recommend you implement a strategy I call BAT—belief audit time. Set a weekly, recurring reminder on your calendar, labeled "BAT," to spend ten minutes, once a week, writing down your beliefs and challenging any limiting ones that pop up. This is your opportunity to go to "BAT" for yourself and your dreams. This is a game changer when done consistently!

There's one more thing I want to share with you about your thoughts and beliefs, and it's the most unlikely but powerful exercise you can imagine.

THANK YOU FOR THAT UNNECESSARY THOUGHT

"It's very simple, Rachel. Just say, 'Thank you for that unnecessary thought,'" my therapist, Wayne, said to me.

Laughing, I asked, "What are you talking about? That makes no sense at all. How is that going to help me not have these thoughts anymore?"

I'd been battling for months with limiting beliefs and fear-ful thoughts concerning my health. At first, I'd tried to ignore my thoughts, but deep down I knew that wasn't the answer. How many times had I reminded myself and others about the importance of acknowledging our mental chatter? I've said on numerous occasions, "Our thoughts and ideas are like little children—they need attention or they'll just keep pestering you."

OUR THOUGHTS AND IDEAS ARE LIKE LITTLE CHILDREN—THEY NEED ATTENTION OR THEY'LL JUST KEEP PESTERING YOU.

#PermissiontoOffend

After taking a three-year hiatus from therapy, I found myself starting to feel wound up pretty tight and decided I finally needed to go back and deal with the post-traumatic stress disorder of the cancer diagnosis as well as the survivor's guilt I was experiencing. During my stay at the cancer treatment center in Mexico, I had bonded with a wonderful group of women, all of whom had passed away within the year. Being the only survivor weighed heavily on my heart, and every time I missed taking my pills or drinking a fresh-pressed green juice, I felt like I was betraying them. Although I was in a few mastermind groups and had a coach to support me, let's keep it real. Coaching is *not* an adequate replacement for therapy with a licensed professional.

A friend highly recommended and connected me with Wayne. He is a kind, gentle soul whose unorthodox approaches to therapy both challenge and amuse me. While I'm completely fascinated by the work of great doctors in the world of cognitive behavioral therapy, mind-set, and positive psychology, Wayne believes we spend too much time thinking about ourselves and our thoughts. His philosophy is that we'd all be much better off if we focused more on outwardly expressing love rather than attempting to process our internal thoughts.

On this particular day, as we went around the merry-go-round of my limiting beliefs for about the fifth time, that's when Wayne said, "It's very simple, Rachel. Just say, 'Thank you for that unnecessary thought.'" He continued with an analogy: "The subconscious mind needs to be approached with humor and gratitude. Picture being at a very fancy restaurant where the table is fully set. You've got the salad fork, dinner fork, soup spoon, butter knife, steak knife, and dessert spoon. As you're eating your meal, a waiter comes up to you and offers you a fork. You don't need the fork. It's unnecessary. So you say to the waiter, 'Thank you for the unnecessary fork.' The waiter, recognizing his mistake, smiles, keeps the fork, and walks away. The fork isn't needed and neither is this thought that keeps coming up for you."

I busted out laughing because it sounded ridiculous. I was legit starting to wonder if Wayne was a real therapist or if he was self-appointed. No lie! Even though I was laughing, I was also quickly pulling up his website to double-check that this man had some credentials and letters behind his name. I'm happy to report that he is indeed licensed and registered with the State of Florida. Phew! Anyhow, I believe in being coachable, so I chose to fully implement Wayne's approach before deciding whether or not it would work.

Over the next week, whenever fear, guilt, or worrisome thoughts entered my mind, I remembered what Wayne had taught me. "Thank you for that unnecessary thought," I would silently say to myself. On days when the thoughts were extra loud, I would audibly repeat, "Thank you for that unnecessary thought." Then I added my own little sprinkle of goodness and began saying, "Thank you for that unnecessary thought. I prefer when you serve me life-affirming thoughts." I figured if my subconscious mind was like a waiter offering up utensils, then putting in a request was worth a try. The following week during my session with Wayne I said, "It's working, Wayne! The scary thoughts are being served up less and less, and better thoughts are being offered. Yay!"

Almost a year has passed since Wayne taught me this practice, and I hardly ever get offered those scary fork thoughts. More and more, I'm served powerful, life-affirming thoughts. I've also shared this concept with many clients and students and they've seen the positive results of this practice as well. Try it for yourself, and remember: the beliefs you hold influence all of your actions and inactions. Ultimately, you are what you believe. Choose wisely and intentionally.

Now that we're done with beliefs, it's time to move to the second part of the identity equation (Beliefs + Values = Identity) and talk about *values*.

VALUES

"Your children are begging for your attention," my friend Linette said with conviction.

She might as well have slapped me in the face for how painful the sting of her words felt. "What?" I asked, trying to stay calm.

"They're starving for your attention. You work too much."

At the time, my daughters were two and four years old, and I was about two years into building my business. Was I in the hustle and grind of an early start-up company? For sure. Were my kids starving for attention? Absolutely not, and I resented every syllable coming out of her judgmental mouth. To say that I was pissed is an understatement. I was enraged.

Linette was a stay-at-home mother, raising two boys. Her entire world revolved around her husband and her children. From the moment her feet hit the floor in the morning until her head hit the pillow at night, everything she did was for them. Breakfast, lunch, housekeeping, laundry, dinner, errands—you name it. If her boys wanted it, Linette did it. Having been raised by a very independent single mom, I couldn't fathom her way of living, and quite frankly I had my own opinions about how she was raising her sons. But I kept it classy and kept my mouth shut. So when she came at me out of left field with her two cents about my babies, I felt a certain type of way. Mainly because after several years of marriage and the multiple identity crises I had endured adjusting to motherhood, I was finally living according to *my* values.

Permission Slip

I give myself permission to live in a world of this *and* that.

#PermissiontoOffend

Our values shift over time, as you'll see in just a moment, and at that time, I valued hard work, having a career, building a legacy, and setting an example for my daughters. I wanted to build something that would provide security for them. I wanted to live according to Proverbs 13:22, which says, "A good person leaves an inheritance for their children's children" (NIV). I wanted to be the example of not just following but also *achieving* my dreams. I believed that I was capable and equipped to be both mom *and* business owner, but I was surrounded by women like Linette who didn't believe having it all was possible. She lived in a this-*or*-that world. I lived (and continue to live) in a world of this *and* that. I have always valued the idea of infinite possibilities, and it's this value system that has allowed me to embody the identity of a woman who lives by deep faith. After all, according to my beliefs, God promises us an abundant life. The books of Exodus, Deuteronomy, Proverbs,

Psalms, and many more have verse after verse detailing how much is available to us.

So confident in my truth was I that without hesitation I fired back, "My children are not starving for attention. They live with both their parents, I play with them, I read to them, and I am also showing them how to pursue their dreams despite the opinions others may have of them."

Now, when I said that last part, I gave her the look. *You know the look.* The one that said, *Go ahead and try me again and see what happens.* Needless to say, the conversation ended abruptly and never again did she offer unsolicited parenting advice. In fact, our friendship flourished. Linette would often watch my daughters for me while I worked, and eventually she hired me as her coach to help get her own business off the ground!

All along, she too had wanted to be true to her identity and follow her dreams and ambitions in addition to motherhood, but no one had ever shown her it was possible. She had been so attached to her role as a mom and wife that it became her identity. Today, Linette is a successful real estate agent *and* an incredible mother to her sons *and* a devoted wife to her husband. She just needed to see what was possible and anchor her own beliefs and values.

TIME TELLS WHERE YOUR VALUES DWELL.

#PermissiontoOffend

What about you? Are you clear on your values, and more important, are you living according to them? You can easily tell by conducting another audit, this time of your activities, with the following alignment opportunity. I call this one a time-value audit. Time tells where your values dwell.

ALIGNMENT OPPORTUNITY

Think about the last twenty-four hours and list all your activities. Go minute by minute, if you can, and write down where you spent your time. Be honest with yourself. Now is not the time for self-judgment, blame, or shame. The goal here is to simply bring things into awareness. If you're really brave, audit the last seven days and see what you come up with.

Note: Don't focus on listing things in order of priority. There's no hierarchy on this list.

What did you discover? Were you working? Were you on social media? If you count social media as part of your job, be honest with yourself: Were you engaged in *meaningful* work that actually produced fruit from your labor? Did you create more than you consumed? As you reflect on your list, what are your thoughts and how do they make you feel?

You may have discovered that your time has been spent on things you consider important, or maybe not so important but engaging. If so, this probably left little room for spending time doing things you actually value. If that's your truth, that's okay. I don't know about you, but when I was growing up, no one sat me down to teach me the importance of defining and aligning with my values on a daily basis. Sure, I can recall once or twice doing some kind of values quiz, but it was never ingrained in me to make connecting with my beliefs and values a regular practice. Now it's part of my routine. Each day I write my values at the top of the current page of my journal. This helps me stay aligned with not just my identity but also my goals. Like I suggested you do a few pages ago, once a week—every Monday, to be precise—I go to "BAT" for myself. I write down my beliefs and challenge any limiting beliefs that pop up. Once a month I also do a time-value audit. These practices are incredibly powerful and eye-opening.

Once I did a time-value audit and to my horror discovered that although I *said* I valued my family over work, my calendar had been overcommitted with work. Quality time with my family had taken a major back seat. Even though I was in the habit of writing down my values daily, I had allowed my value of consistency to trump my value of family. As you practice embodying your values, you might discover they shift according to your season in life. This is why creating daily and monthly practices makes such a big difference.

ALIGNMENT OPPORTUNITY

Pull it all together.

What do I believe?

What do I value?

What do I stand for?

What do I stand against?

Why does it matter to me?

How do I want to show up today?

Likewise, routinely writing your beliefs and values helps you stay in consistent connection with your true identity. When it comes time to speak your piece or stand your ground, there will be little or no hesitation. You'll *know* who you are, what you stand for, why it matters, and how you want to show up.

THE INCEPTION OF SELF-REJECTION

"Her mother died of AIDS too."

My playful skip came to a full and complete stop. I looked toward the stoop of my dad's apartment building to see my stepmother pointing me out to some random neighbor. Did you know that if the world suddenly stopped spinning, tornado-like winds would engulf us and the earth would massively quake, causing an indescribable catastrophe? That's the best description I can give you to express the magnitude of how crushed my soul felt hearing those words.

"What?! No, she didn't! My mother died of pneumonia, and I have her death certificate to prove it," I fired back at my stepmother. A million thoughts raced through my twelve-year-old mind as I tried to make sense of what she had said. *She's lying. She's just trying to hurt me. She always does this whenever I come over. She finds some way to mess with me.*

On a very rare occasion, I was visiting my father and his bi— Nope, I'm not gonna do it. Not today. That would be an insult to female dogs around the world anyway. I was visiting my father and his new wife. Period. She was a cutthroat woman who always found a way to take digs at me. Maybe it was because I was rebellious. Maybe it was because I was an early riser and both she and my dad were night owls who were inconvenienced by my childish morning needs, like breakfast and a good-morning hug. Maybe it was because she was jealous of a dead woman, and I, a carbon copy of my mother, was a reminder of the woman she would never live up to. Maybe it was just because she was evil. I'll go with the latter, but whatever.

Regardless of her motives, on that bright, sunny afternoon, while skipping around and enjoying the carefree nature of summer days, my foundation was rocked, *again!*

Wasn't it enough that my biological mother had died when I was three and a half years old?

Wasn't it enough that one day my father dropped me off at my godmother's house and just left me there?

I was finally starting to enjoy some stability and security in my life. And now this? The defamation of my dead mother to some neighborhood stranger? No! Hell no! I wasn't gonna stand for it.

"You're a liar!" I continued. "You're just jealous because my dad loved her more than he loves you." I threw out whatever painful words I could sling her way. I wanted her to hurt just as badly as I was hurting. And then she did it—she threw a machete into my heart and killed the last remnants of whatever childhood I had left.

"Your mother died of AIDS, and your father has it too. He's gonna die just like she did!" she said with a venomous look in her eyes. Ooh, she was evil.

"What?! LIARRRRRR! YOU'RE A LIAR!" I screamed and ran into the courtyard and up to the apartment.

"Daaaa-ddddy! YOU LIED TO ME! You all lied to me!" I cried hysterically. Hot tears burned my face as I tried to make sense of what had just happened.

"What are you talking about, Loi?" Loi was a made-up name my dad and biological mother had come up with when I was a baby. He was Daddy Loi, she was Mama Loi, and I was Baby Loi.

"You all told me Mama Loi died of natural causes, but Margie just told me she died of AIDS and you have it too and you're gonna die just like she did. You lied to me!" I sobbed uncontrollably. My father's expression shifted from confusion to a rage I had never seen before. Up until that point, I had never really seen my father get angry, except for the one time I cut my own bangs. Even then, he didn't look the way he looked as I stood there crying.

His forehead scrunched up and his eyebrows furrowed as Margie walked into the apartment. That day—the day I found out my father was dying—was the day I saw a whole new side of Ventura Rodriguez. Vinnie (government name: Ventura), my father, was an incredibly patient, fun, and loving character. He was talented in all the arts. He was a great sketch artist, played various musical instruments, and was a gifted and articulate writer who loved to build model sailboats and strum on his guitar for hours. There was never a bad time when Vinnie was around. But Ventura was a whole other character. This dude didn't mess around. I had never met this version of my dad, but secretly, *I liked him.*

Because while Vinnie did whatever his wife told him to do, even if she was hurting me or my sister, Ventura didn't take her sh*t. He went off! "Rachel, go to the bedroom," he said, staring straight through me and into his wife. Trying to pull myself together so she couldn't see my heartache, I sniffled my way into the only bedroom in the apartment. As I did so, I heard him scream, "What did you tell her?"

Nonchalantly, like the heartless being she was, she answered, "The truth. She needed to know anyway."

They continued to argue back and forth, with my father taking tones and using language I had never heard him use before, as I lay there in the fetal position, silently crying in bed. I don't remember word-for-word the exchange or the conversation my dad and I had once he calmed down. But I do remember feeling confused, inse-cure, and doubtful of everything I knew to be true. *How could my mother have died of AIDS? I have her death certificate. It says in plain English, "Cause of death: Natural causes." Is this just a cruel joke? Is my biological mother even dead at all, or did she give me away because she didn't want me?*

I rattled through these questions over and over again.

That Sunday my dad took me back to my house via the train, and each time I saw a petite brunette woman with blue eyes, I found myself wondering, *Are you my mom? Did you give me up? Are you still alive, and do you miss me?*

When I got home, I confronted my mom. "Mommy, is it true? Did my mother die of AIDS?" She didn't hesitate or sugarcoat. "Yes. It's true." She said something after that, but I couldn't hear her words. Earth was screeching to a full and complete stop again. Even though deep down I knew Margie had been telling the truth, a part of me still held out hope that this was all just one of her nasty tricks. I was hoping my mom would tell me it was all a lie. The hands of time would be reversed and I could go back to when my dad was healthy and my biological mom had just randomly died young.

"How could you keep this from me? How can this even be true when we have her death certificate?" I walked to my room to pull out the last remaining shred of evidence to prove this was all a terrible misunderstanding. She followed me and said, "Back then, they didn't really know what AIDS was, and if you put it on the death certificate, you couldn't get a funeral home to prepare the body. That's why she had a closed-casket funeral. No one knew how it was spread or if it died with the body." A nurse for more than two decades, she spoke like she would to a colleague or a patient, not to her heartbroken daughter.

"And Daddy has it too?" I asked with hope the size of a grain of sand that she would say no.

"Yes. Your father has it too."

I broke down once again, sinking onto my bed. This was too much to take in. *What did I do to deserve this? Why is my life one bad thing after another? When is it going to get better?* "Wait a minute," I said, looking up at her. "Does this mean I have it too? Am I going to die like them?" I buried my face in my hands, fresh tears pouring like a faucet.

"No. You don't have it. You were tested twice as a baby," she said calmly as she sat down on the bed, wrapping her arms around me.

"You *tested* me?" Panic surged through my body. *What is going on? What else did they do to me without me knowing? Was I part of an experiment? Is life real or is someone watching my life play out on a television screen somewhere in the cosmos?*

"Deep breaths, Rachel. Deep breaths. Try to calm down," she coaxed.

Calm down? Easy for her to say. No one has been lying to her for her entire life. Nevertheless, I knew she was right. I needed to pull it together, because now that I knew the truth, I needed to figure out how to move forward. Trying to regain my composure, I sat up straight and took a few deep breaths. "So what does this all mean?"

"It doesn't mean anything, Rachel. Nothing has changed. Your father loves you very much. I love you very much. He's still here. I'm still here. Nothing has changed except that now you know. But you are safe. You are healthy, and that's all that matters."

Her words brought little comfort. My head was still spinning. Everything I had known to be true up to that point was now in question. What parts of my life were real and what parts had been conveniently made up or covered up?

This was the trauma that flipped the on switch for my self-rejection. Remember I told you in the beginning of this book, self-rejection is what we do as a coping mechanism to help us feel safe. Discovering the lies I had been told created a deep wound in my identity. I didn't know who I was or whom I could trust. The stories I told myself were pieced together by the evidence of my experiences.

Everyone I love lies to me.

Everyone I love leaves me.

Everyone whose love I crave rejects me.

The pain of that moment was so unbearable, I began to self-reject in a variety of ways to cope with the trauma. It was also my way of protecting myself from being rejected and abandoned again. I would reject myself before anyone else did. Sometimes my self-rejection looked like judgment or being overly critical of my body, while other times it looked like me abandoning great opportunities. Even though I *loved* dancing with a passion, I remember quitting dance class the year after getting accepted into a prominent dance school in New York City. As I got older, self-rejection presented itself in my life through disordered eating, alcohol abuse, and lots of career sabotage. Ever been there?

My story may feel mega traumatic to you, or maybe, compared to your own story, mine is a walk in the park. Here's the good thing: no one is keeping score, and one person's experience doesn't minimize or maximize the other's. Life, from its inception, is predisposed to be laced with trauma. These experiences can sometimes lead us to adopt identities outside our truth, not just because we aren't sure of who we are but also because we're looking for ways to keep ourselves safe and protected. For example, if an outgoing, talkative child is punished in her home for speaking when grownups are conversing, this child might take on the identity of a shy or quiet person who doesn't speak unless spoken to. By staying silent, the child avoids punishment, disconnection, and rejection in the home, but this also carries on outside the home and into adulthood. She had to stay quiet to be accepted, and the belief that silence equals safety became encoded in her identity. Deep down, though, her true identity was also someone who had big, bold ideas and lots to say.

Not speaking and living in your truth is a form of self-rejection that tells your subconscious, *I'm not worthy.* This is why it was so important for you to take the time to examine your beliefs and values and find the source of these thoughts. Let me be the first to say that the realization of engaging in self-rejection behavior can be painful. One might even be tempted to argue, "I know I'm worthy. That's not my issue." If that's your truth, okay, and also, *are you sure about that?* Or have you been weathered so hard by life that you're afraid if you actually own up to the fact that somewhere deep down you don't feel worthy, it might be the admission that brings you to your knees? Maybe you're like my best friend, who will often say, "Uh-uh. I don't have time to fall apart today. Go take that somewhere else," whenever I offer up a coaching question that will force her to get honest and examine the most intimate parts of her life—the scary parts that dwell in the darkest corners of her mind.

Wherever you stand, this is your invitation right now to dig deeper, because in the next chapter I'm going to introduce you to the Offender Identity Framework, and knowing where you've self-rejected (if ever) will help you determine where you might land in the framework.

Before you move on, take a moment to affirm yourself.

─────**AFFIRMATION**─────

I KNOW WHO I AM, WHAT I STAND FOR, AND WHY IT MATTERS. I KNOW EXACTLY HOW I WANT TO SHOW UP TODAY.

──────────── #PermissiontoOffend ────

PRINCIPLES OF ANCHORING YOUR IDENTITY

- ❯ You get to validate and disprove your beliefs and values on a daily basis.
- ❯ Your beliefs amplify your identity.
- ❯ Shame is not who you are. Shame is the feeling produced from taking (or not taking) actions that don't align with your true identity. No one can shame you unless you let them.
- ❯ A limiting belief is a state of mind or conviction that you think to be true but limits you in some way.
- ❯ Thank your unnecessary thoughts and request life-affirming thoughts.
- ❯ Your values can and will shift based on your current season in life. Go to "BAT" for yourself by writing down your beliefs weekly to ensure you're staying in alignment to your true identity.
- ❯ Conducting a monthly time-value audit is powerful and eye-opening.
- ❯ Self-rejection is what we do as a coping mechanism to help us feel safe. Traumatic life experiences can sometimes lead us to adopt identities outside our truth, not just because we aren't sure of who we are but also because we're looking for ways to feel safe and protected.

Can you see the importance of taking this time to anchor your identity? You examined your beliefs and values didn't you? You *know* who you are. You are not the mistakes you have made. You are not the weight you carry or have lost. You are the sum of your beliefs and values. That's it. Nothing more, nothing less. With this knowledge and confidence, you get to start living unfiltered, unashamed, and unafraid—you get to be as powerful as you choose to be!

This is the kind of work that should be revisited often. Just like one might partake in spring cleaning, make sure you come back to this section and dust off any residue left behind from past imposed values and beliefs. And remember to be on the lookout for newly adopted values and beliefs that don't actually serve you. Thems the tricky ones because they look so good. These are the small action steps that create massive results and get you closer to living unfiltered, unashamed, and unafraid!

4

BECOME THE
EMPATHETIC OFFENDER

I have a confession: I used to *love* reality TV. Okay, correction: I still love reality TV, but I've mostly graduated from the scandalosas of the Real Housewives franchise to HGTV, Food Network, and DIY shows. Because hello, I'm an adult. Also, I love the inspiration I get from my more sophisticated viewing choices. However, there was a time when I had a standing weekly appointment on my calendar with all the housewives of every city. During one *Real Housewives of Atlanta: Reunion*, NeNe Leakes and Kandi Burruss were really going at it. Finally, NeNe said with authority and conviction, "I said what I said." To which Kandi responded, "Well, what you said was some bullsh*t." The women carried on arguing, and although I can't remember how it ended, I do recall that NeNe made absolutely no apology whatsoever for her actions despite Kandi's multiple attempts to express how upset she was. NeNe's "I said what I said" became a viral meme that is still in high circulation.

My goal for you with this book is that you give yourself permission to offend and speak with the same level of conviction as NeNe but to do so with compassion and empathy. That's what you'll learn as you continue to work through this book. Living an unfiltered life is the product of leading with empathy.

EMPATHY IS THE ABILITY TO UNDERSTAND AND SHARE THE FEELINGS OF OTHERS.

#PermissiontoOffend

Empathy is the ability to understand and share the feelings of others. As we delve into our journey toward a *Permission to Offend* lifestyle, it's important to understand that the way you speak your truth without hurting others is by tapping into an empathetic nature. This enables you to know, feel, connect, and, if necessary, move to help others without taking ownership of their stories. By tapping into empathy, you'll be able to "offend" more freely because you'll be speaking your truth with a higher degree of love, compassion, and understanding for the other person. If NeNe would have taken just a few minutes to consider Kandi's perspective, the conversation could have gone better. Sometimes our words and actions hurt others not because of what we said or did but because we didn't take the time to hold space for their emotional experience.

Think about a time when you've called a friend to vent, and instead of listening and holding space, she launched into an I-told-you-so monologue or a story of her own. The problem wasn't her unsolicited speech—if she's right she's right, and you're big enough to admit it—it was that she didn't give you the space to process and feel your feelings first.

Being empathetic means being able to *understand* from the other person's point of view. You don't have to agree, own, or take on what the other person is saying, doing, or feeling. But being able to understand why or how they got to where they are is an indication of your ability to empathize. In the *Reunion* exchange, it appeared as though NeNe didn't take any time to consider Kandi's position.

Real talk: I get it. When I'm pissed and in my feelings about something, the last thing I want to do is empathize with the person pissing me off. Before I started embodying the *Permission to Offend* lifestyle, whenever I was upset, the first thing I'd want to do is *fight*. Maybe not physically, although (not proud to admit) I have gotten into a few physical scuffles in my yesteryears. But I'd definitely want to scream, yell, and curse everyone and their mama out. *Now* when I'm truly upset, hurt, mad, angry, whatever, I do still scream—I'm not gonna lie. But I don't scream *at* the person. Rather, I process my emotions by using the Framework for Freedom you practiced in chapter 1. I then remind myself of my beliefs, values, and identity, and finally, I lean into my empathetic skills. I still speak my mind and share my truth, only there is less wounded offense. We'll talk more about that in a bit.

What I want to do right now is make sure you don't confuse "empathy" with "sympathy." Brené Brown eloquently distinguishes the two words by saying, "Empathy fuels connection. Sympathy drives disconnection."* Empathy says, *I understand your truth*. Sympathy says, *I'm sorry about your truth*.

If you have ever been in a situation in which the other person was unable to empathize with where you were coming from, then I think you'll appreciate where we're going next. You're going to learn the Offender Identity Framework, the four identities, and the hurdles, lessons, and affirmations for each identity. That's a lot of "identity" talk, I know. The work will challenge and stretch you, but I think that's why you're here. Because you're ready to experience more freedom, and that's exactly the result of mastering this framework. Let's get into it.

---

* Brené Brown, "The Power of Vulnerability—Brené Brown," RSA (Royal Society of Arts), YouTube video, 21:47, posted August 15, 2013, https://www.youtube.com /watch?v=sXSjc-pbXk4&t=0s.

OFFENDER IDENTITY FRAMEWORK

Like superheroes in our own blockbuster movie, we all put on a special suit to protect us against the forces of evil in the world. Okay, maybe I'm being a little dramatic. But it's kind of true. We become who we need to be in order to stay "safe," and avoid the big three: *judgment, rejection,* and *defamation.* The fear and avoidance of these three experiences is what keeps us from speaking our truth, walking in faith, and living in freedom. We wear the identity that fits the situation to ensure others won't judge, reject, or defame us. For example, growing up in a Puerto Rican household, I was taught to speak only when spoken to. For a loudmouth like myself, this was a rule that I frequently challenged. That is until the day I inserted myself into a grown-up conversation and my mother, giving me *the look,* leaned over and whispered, *"Yo te cojo en casa."* A chill still runs up my spine as I remember that day. *"Yo te cojo en casa"* means something like "I'll get you when we get home." And get me she did! Oooh weee, my mama lit me up. *Never, ever* again did I speak when adults were speaking. In fact, after that experience, even when adults spoke directly to me, I would look at my mom to get her approval before opening my mouth. This became an automatic self-preservation response that took years to turn off.

Permission Slip

I give myself permission to take up space and speak up!

#PermissiontoOffend

You may not have ever experienced *the look,* but I'm sure you've had some situation in your life that has caused you to be just a little less yourself. Maybe you've been in a position where you've had to dim your light or put your needs and wants on hold. Whatever you've experienced in the past, you can overcome this response by learning how to embody the identity of the Empathetic Offender.

The requirement is first to learn how to operate in high levels of faith and personal truth. After completing the identity work in chapters 2 and 3, you should be clear and confident in what you believe. It's okay if you're still trying on new beliefs and values— remember, every season produces new ideologies for both. The next step is to layer in faith so you can stand by those beliefs and values as you walk in your personal truth. To make sure you and I are on the same page, let's define terms:

FAITH: complete trust and confidence in someone or something.

OBJECTIVE TRUTH: the actual state of the matter.

PERSONAL TRUTH: what you have chosen to believe despite the opinions, thoughts, or evidence presented by others.

When I'm in full connection with my Empathetic Offender identity, which you'll learn more about in just a moment, I'm very comfortable saying out loud, "Jesus Christ is my Lord and Savior." Making that statement requires two levels of deep faith. First, faith to believe and accept the story as personal truth; the objective truth is, Jesus was a man in the Bible. Secondly, faith to say it out loud at the risk of offending or triggering someone or (worse) being told that speaking my faith is proselytizing. (Lean in for a secret: One of my biggest fears was being called a Bible thumper. Agh! I can't! Make it stop. Let's move on.)

I kind of got ahead of myself, talking about the Empathetic Offender identity. I love and respect that identity so much that I wanted to tell you all about it immediately, if not sooner. But there are three other identities in the framework I have to share with you first.

The Offender Identity Framework is divided into four quadrants. Each quadrant depicts a level of personal truth and faith, as reflected on the x-axis and y-axis (see the following image). You'll read the term "low personal truth," which is not synonymous with "inauthentic." Instead, operating in low personal truth is when you engage in actions that are not necessarily aligned to your values or beliefs in order to meet your needs for the moment. You'll also see the term "low faith," which is how you show up when you don't believe in yourself or lack the courage to show up fully self-expressed.

Looking at the framework, in the top left quadrant, I present to you, the Critic.

THE CRITIC IDENTITY

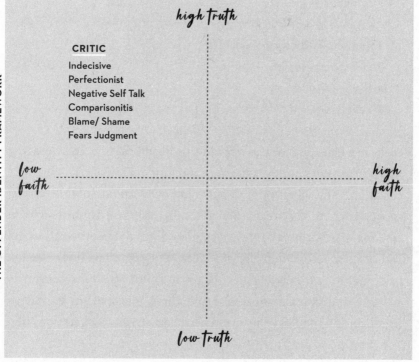

This identity is present when you're in high personal truth and low faith. If you've been in your Critic identity, you probably over-think *a lot*. This is you if you know your truth but have a hard time sharing it freely. You are so plagued by the fear of being rejected, removed, or even—dare I say it—#canceled that instead of speaking your truth, you say nothing. You make excuses and ultimately default to criticizing and judging yourself as well as others quite harshly. If you are in the Critic identity, you might even find that you gaslight yourself. If you're not familiar with the term, gaslighting is "making someone question their own reality." In this case, if you've ever found yourself wondering, *Wait, was I wrong?* even when you knew in your heart of hearts you were right, you might have been gaslighting yourself.

CHARACTERISTICS OF THE CRITIC

▶ Is indecisive
▶ Is prone to perfectionism
▶ Tends toward negative self-talk
▶ Has comparison-itis
▶ Blames/shames
▶ Fears judgment

I once had a client who *lived* in this quadrant. She knew exactly what she wanted and was deeply rooted in her values. During our coaching calls, her bright, water-blue eyes would sparkle as she spoke about her big dreams and goals. In other words, she had high personal truth. She would take copious notes during the call as we laid out her action steps for the week. But just a few hours would pass, and lo and behold, she'd begin to spiral down into negative self-talk and comparison-itis. From there, she'd begin to waffle in indecision, and on the rare chance when she took action, her perfectionism would stunt her progress. I really felt for her because I knew just how badly she wanted to achieve success on her terms, but the Critic in her continued to hold her back.

By coaching her through the Framework for Freedom (chapter 1), we were able to identify where her patterns of perfectionism, negative self-talk, and comparison-itis came from. Turns out she had a memory of painting plates with her grandmother that did not go well. Her grandmother was a bit of a perfectionist herself, and when my client didn't paint the plate exactly as her grandmother wanted, she was pushed aside and told she had done it "wrong." From that moment, she fiercely held on to the story that everything had to be perfect; otherwise, she'd be cast aside.

The story doesn't end there. Although she loved her grandmother, this exchange created deep seeds of resentment for my client. As we continued to work through the alignment opportunities I've outlined for you in this book, my client was able to make amends with her grandmother, break the pattern, and shift into high personal truth *and* high faith. Today, my client is taking consistent action, honoring her truth, and giving herself permission to do things perfectly imperfectly!

THE PLEASER IDENTITY

In the lower left quadrant, operating in low personal truth and low faith, is the Pleaser.

If you're the Pleaser, most likely you've been scared, shy, or timid. You *know*, but you have trouble *believing*. As soon as the Pleaser starts to take one step forward, she goes three steps back. Often she will hide or find ways to deflect or minimize her truth. On occasion, the Pleaser will take a stand but will then very quickly walk it back, or go into hiding before anyone sees her. The Pleaser is the chameleon of the group. She's able to morph into whomever she needs to be in order to fit in and stay safe in the moment.

THE OFFENDER IDENTITY FRAMEWORK

high truth

CRITIC

Indecisive
Perfectionist
Negative Self Talk
Comparisonitis
Blame/ Shame
Fears Judgment

low faith

high faith

PLEASER

Breaks Boundaries
Low Self-Integrity
Has influence but no authority
Fears rejection and defamation
Negative Self-Talk
False starts
Guilt/fear

low truth

CHARACTERISTICS OF THE PLEASER

▶ Breaks boundaries with oneself and others
▶ Has low self-integrity and often breaks promises
   to oneself
▶ Tends toward negative self-talk
▶ Is inauthentic
▶ Is a false starter
▶ Displays guilt and/or fear

After more than a year of thinking about it, Iviana finally had the courage to launch her podcast *Grace for Breakfast*. A few episodes into her show, she decided to record a series on forgiveness. One of the episodes in the series was on self-forgiveness. Within a week or so of the episode airing, a member of her church sent Iviana a private message on social media, saying, "I listened to your podcast and I don't agree because as Christians we are not supposed to forgive ourselves." Confused by his message, Iviana sent her podcast to a close friend to get a second opinion. To her shock and dismay, the friend agreed with the man and reiterated the same belief—under no circumstances are Christians to forgive themselves. In her own words, Iviana said, "After my girlfriend put me in my place, I felt very uncomfortable sharing my podcast with a certain group of religious people, and I felt uncomfortable sharing my beliefs on the podcast, and it made me kind of water it down to accommodate other people."

Not only did she water down her podcast but also the loss of faith in her abilities and the show itself caused Iviana to quit after only two seasons. The good news is that she followed all the steps outlined in this book and decided she was ready to go back to her love. You can tune in to *Grace for Breakfast* wherever all podcasts are streamed. Iviana has committed to giving herself permission to offend, so you won't find any watered down content there!

Quick side note before we move on to the next offender identity: Self-forgiveness is some of the most powerful and healing work you can do. I understand the thought process of the two individuals who criticized Iviana, however the Bible says to forgive others for their transgressions (Matt. 6:14). As you'll see in the next chapter, sometimes *you* are your biggest transgressor. Also, the Bible specifically says, "Judge not, that you be not judged" (Matt. 7:1, NKJV). Listen, friends, Christians are fallible human beings—we're not all self-righteous. So please, give yourself permission to forgive your-self! Okay, I said what I said. Moving on.

THE WOUNDED OFFENDER IDENTITY

Throughout my life I've vacillated between being the Critic and the Pleaser, but the identity I've most often worn is that of the Wounded Offender. I've fought fights that weren't mine because I was so out-raged by injustice. I've often reacted impulsively, never considering the consequences or how others might be hurt by my words. I've sim-ply charged forward into battle with no care or concern for anything other than my agenda. Because that's what the Wounded Offender does. If you recall the example from *The Real Housewives of Atlanta: Reunion*, NeNe Leakes was the classic Wounded Offender.

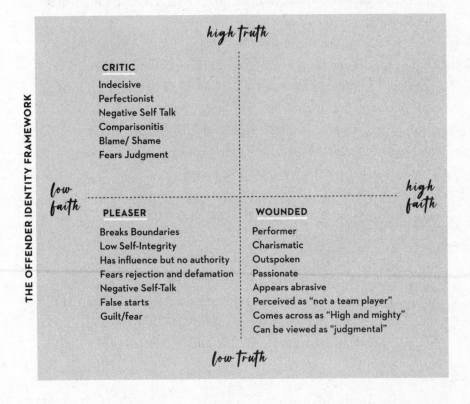

THE OFFENDER IDENTITY FRAMEWORK

high truth

CRITIC
Indecisive
Perfectionist
Negative Self Talk
Comparisonitis
Blame/ Shame
Fears Judgment

low faith   *high faith*

PLEASER
Breaks Boundaries
Low Self-Integrity
Has influence but no authority
Fears rejection and defamation
Negative Self-Talk
False starts
Guilt/fear

WOUNDED
Performer
Charismatic
Outspoken
Passionate
Appears abrasive
Perceived as "not a team player"
Comes across as "High and mighty"
Can be viewed as "judgmental"

low truth

Operating in low personal truth and high faith, the Wounded Offender, on the surface, might look like the twin sister of the Critic. They share a few characteristics, like blame, shame, and negativity. But unlike the Critic, the Wounded Offender is likely to project out into the world. She has the highest levels of faith and believes her personal truths are universal. In reality, she is incredibly empathetic but comes across as combative because her kindness has been mistaken for weakness far too many times. Often the Wounded Offender identity is worn by someone who has been victimized or is part of a marginalized group and is a champion for justice. The burden and weight of all she's endured is so heavy that she must speak out and take radical action regardless of the impact.

CHARACTERISTICS OF THE WOUNDED OFFENDER

▶ Is outspoken

▶ Is passionate

▶ Appears abrasive

▶ Is perceived as "not a team player"

▶ Can come across as "high and mighty"

▶ Can be viewed as "judgmental"

Interestingly, this identity not only appears during seasons of conflict but also shows up in relationships, as it did for my friend Veronica.

Veronica had been going through a dry spell. Ladies, you know what I'm talking about—involuntary celibacy (wink, wink). We were chatting on the phone when she confessed, "Girl, I'm in heat. I need to get laid. This can't be life!" We giggled and I didn't think much of it until about a week later, when I got a text. "I got laid. Can the congregation say amen?"

I literally laughed out loud and sent her a "Weppppaaaaaa and Amen!" response. *Wepa* is the Puerto Rican equivalent of "Woohoo" but way better.

Anyhow, another week later we were chatting again when I asked about her new beau. It turns out she met him on a dating app notoriously known for no strings attached hookups. She told me something felt off about him and that she wasn't sure he had even given her his real name. I pressed for more details, and she said, "I couldn't 'find his name tied to anything, and he told me his wife was dead."

Immediately I screamed out loud, "He's lying!! I watch a lot of investigative discovery TV and that's the number one lie crazy men give."

When I asked why she was still messing with this guy who was clearly lying, she said, "He's just my in-the-meantime, in-between-time guy."

"But is that what you really want?" I asked.

"NOPE! I want a fine mofo who's obsessed with me, who can rub my feet, who can stimulate my mind, who is emotionally healthy, and has all his teeth." She was laughing, but I could feel the pain in her soul. She wanted her true match and was so tired of playing these games. But it was her Wounded Offender that had opened the app and swiped right on this guy who was clearly below her desired standards. In this case, Veronica was operating in low personal truth to satisfy her needs in the moment. The problem is that all the time and energy Veronica expends on this guy takes up the space available for her true match.

I have deep empathy for the Wounded Offender because not only do I identify with her personally but I also know that if she tapped into the heart and soul of her truth, she could channel all that energy, attract the desires of her heart, *and* be a real champion for change.

Check in: Have you seen yourself in any of these identities so far? Can you think of a time when you've bounced between identities to fit the needs of the situation? If you're someone who feels a strong negative response to labels, try looking at the framework without the names and simply focus on the characteristics within each quadrant.

Your goal, if you're going to embody the attributes and characteristics needed to give yourself permission to offend, is to practice living in high personal truth *and* high faith. Which leads us to . . .

THE EMPATHETIC OFFENDER IDENTITY

The Empathetic Offender is someone who shows empathy for themselves as well as others. An Empathetic Offender also shows grace. When you're operating in this identity, you respond before you react. You're willing to speak up and share your truth, even if it means having hard conversations. You're willing to stand up for what you believe in and take risks for the sake of your personal truth and that of others.

THE OFFENDER IDENTITY FRAMEWORK

high truth

CRITIC	**EMPATHETIC**
Indecisive	Deeply rooted in identity
Perfectionist	Charismatic
Negative Self Talk	Outspoken
Comparisonitis	Passionate
Blame/ Shame	Appears abrasive
Fears Judgment	Perceived as "not a team player"
	Comes across as "High and mighty"
	Can be viewed as "judgmental"
PLEASER	**WOUNDED**
Breaks Boundaries	Performer
Low Self-Integrity	Charismatic
Has influence but no authority	Outspoken
Fears rejection and defamation	Passionate
Negative Self-Talk	Appears abrasive
False starts	Perceived as "not a team player"
Guilt/fear	Comes across as "High and mighty"
	Can be viewed as "judgmental"

low faith ··· *high faith*

low truth

CHARACTERISTICS OF THE EMPATHETIC OFFENDER

▶ Is deeply rooted in their identity

▶ Is understanding

▶ Has a strong sense of belief in oneself

▶ Is able to hold space for beliefs contrary to their own
without forfeiting their own truth

▶ Can be compassionate

▶ Tends to be firm

▶ Is honorable

▶ Seeks justice

▶ Stands up for others without compromising oneself

An Empathetic Offender does and says things others might perceive as offensive if it were not for their ability to do so with dignity and respect for the people involved. An Empathetic Offender says what needs to be said, does what needs to be done, and does so without compromising their own values or beliefs. Period.

ALIGNMENT OPPORTUNITY

Now that you better understand the Offender Identity Framework, which of these four identities have you *most often* embodied? Or which quadrant have you defaulted to the most? It's okay to identify with more than one. Which feels most dominant now?

What would being an Empathetic Offender mean to you, and how can you embody that identity today? Make a list of at least three ways you can start to live as an Empathetic Offender. (Four examples: *Ask more questions to gain understanding, Listen intently, Express compassion,* and *Hold a firm boundary.*)

Who or what (organization, institution, or cause) benefits from you stepping into your identity as an Empathetic Offender?

Next, I want to offer you some tools to help you move along the quadrants and take up permanent residence in the Empathetic Offender corner. Understanding the unique hurdles each identity has to overcome might give you a better sense of how to quickly hop, skip, and jump your way over to the top right corner.

IDENTITY HURDLES, LESSONS, AND AFFIRMATIONS

The following *hurdles* are the unique challenges each identity must overcome in order to move through the quadrants. Your opportunity is to recognize when you're presented with the challenge and take fast action.

The *lessons* are the positive attributes of that identity that you can bring with you across the Offender Identity Framework.

The *affirmations* are the anchors you can use to remind yourself that the Empathetic Offender quadrant is actually the best position you can be in to walk in truth, faith, and freedom. This is also where you get to live unfiltered, unashamed, and unafraid.

THE CRITIC

HIGH PERSONAL TRUTH, LOW FAITH

HURDLES: To make decisions without second-guessing. To end comparing oneself to others. To reduce negative self-talk.

LESSON: Practice self-compassion. Where do you need to forgive yourself and others?

AFFIRMATION: *It's safe for me to speak my truth without blame or shame.*

THE PLEASER

LOW PERSONAL TRUTH, LOW FAITH

HURDLES: To take a stand for or against what you believe. To seek verification instead of validation (more on this in chapter 6).

LESSON: Get clear on your truth and lean into it. What do you believe? What do you value? Honor all of it.

AFFIRMATION: *When I speak my truth, I pave the way for others to do the same.*

THE WOUNDED OFFENDER

LOW PERSONAL TRUTH, HIGH FAITH

HURDLE: To release victimhood without denying the harm you've endured.

LESSON: Review the stories of your life and find the truth of who you were before you had to protect yourself and others. Begin to lead with the truth of your identity.

AFFIRMATION: *I am seen, heard, and better understood when I stand up for my beliefs with empathy and compassion for all.*

THE EMPATHETIC OFFENDER

HIGH PERSONAL TRUTH, HIGH FAITH

Note that although the Empathetic Offender identity is your goal, I want to also highlight that this quadrant isn't without its own unique hurdle, lesson, and affirmation. So I've included it to show you that every identity has its work cut out.

HURDLE: To let go of taking ownership or responsibility for someone else's truth in an attempt to be empathetic or compassionate.

LESSON: Justice requires truth and accountability. Where can you hold yourself more accountable as you walk in the identity of empathetic offense?

AFFIRMATION: *It's safe for me to offend in defense of my truth when I do so with empathy and compassion.*

Play around with the identities you feel most aligned with and practice overcoming the hurdles, adopting the lessons, and repeating the affirmations. In order to move forward and overcome the emotion associated with the "I feel stuck" mentality, we must do things to help us grow. This is growth work! Time to get unstuck and start speaking and living your truth.

———— **AFFIRMATION** ————

I AM AN EMPATHETIC OFFENDER. I LIVE MY TRUTH AND HOLD SPACE FOR OTHERS TO DO THE SAME.

———————— #PermissiontoOffend ————

PERMISSION TO OFFEND PRINCIPLES

▶ Empathy is the ability to understand and share the feelings of others.

▶ Automatic self-preservation causes us to become who we need to be in order to stay safe.

▶ Personal truth is what you have chosen to believe despite the opinions, thoughts, or evidence presented by others.

▶ Operating in low personal truth is not synonymous with being inauthentic. Rather, you are engaging in actions that are not aligned with your values or beliefs in order to meet your needs in the moment.

▶ It's normal to see yourself in one or all of the identities in the framework.

We've *all* volleyed between the identities in the framework. They are identities we've had to take on to stay "safe." That's okay. Now that you know and understand each one, you can be more intentional and practice being an Empathetic Offender.

That's the identity that helps you live in your highest personal truth and also allows you to walk in deeper faith, which leads to total freedom. And let me say this about freedom: not everyone *wants* to be free. I know that may sound crazy, but legitimately, there are people who choose to live in the prisons of their own stories, fears, judgments, and limiting beliefs. As you start walking in your Empathetic Offender identity, those people will most likely be triggered. They may also be the ones who potentially judge, reject, and defame you. I'm not saying it *will* happen, but it *might*. I want you to be prepared. What's coming up will help you get and *stay* ready for all that you might face as you aim for your highest personal truth as well as high faith.

PART 2

I GIVE MYSELF PERMISSION TO LIVE IN FAITH

Be on guard. Stand firm in the faith. Be courageous. Be strong.

—1 CORINTHIANS 16:13, NLT

5

WALK IN OFFENSE

Angie, a client who is now a dear friend and one of my inspirations for writing this book, sent me an interesting text message of self-discovery. We had worked together on and off for three years, and in that time I had watched and supported her as she made the transformation from an introverted, restrained, and struggling entrepreneur to a self-assured, six-figure-earning CEO. She had grown leaps and bounds not just in business but also in her personal life, but she still had some lingering struggles. (I mean seriously, though, don't we all?)

"OMG! Boundaries are extremely difficult for me! I'm afraid of rejection. Boundaries are an open door for people to walk away and show me what I fear the most: that I'm not as important to them as they are to me and that I'm replaceable."

Ouch! I could tell she was having a tough time processing this awareness. I also wasn't surprised to see that boundaries were still such an issue. When we first started out on our journey together, Angie was a classic Pleaser who has since graduated to mostly Empathetic Offender with an occasional cameo from her Critic identity. For the most part, she now speaks her truth, puts herself out there, and tackles scary goals. But every now and then, her Critic identity shows up and boundaries become a major issue for her. By the way, whether your most recurring identity is the Critic, the Pleaser, or the Wounded Offender, you've likely found yourself compromising boundaries here and there. This breach of boundaries is detrimental to living a fully self-expressed life of high personal truth and high faith. Those of us who embrace and embody the identity of the Empathetic Offender understand that boundaries are nonnegotiable.

I considered not including this chapter because there are *so many* other books piled high on shelves that teach the importance of boundaries and how to set them. And yet the number of people who still struggle with this issue is alarming. What's the holdup? What's it gonna take for (the collective) you to get it together, set a boundary, and honor the darn thing? Seriously! Let's *get. It. To-ge-ther.*

But even as I hear those words bouncing around in my head, I know we require multiple exposures to a concept or idea before it breaks through the subconscious–conscious barrier and into our awareness. Even then, much more is required than just reading a book and doing a few exercises. You have to *decide* you are going to be the kind of person who loves and respects yourself so much that honoring your boundaries is an act of self-care.

Permission Slip

I give myself permission to make honoring my boundaries an act of self-care.

#PermissiontoOffend

Setting and honoring boundaries is more than just guarding your time and energy; it's about protecting your peace and preserving your health. When we don't honor and protect our boundaries, it can often result in emotional suppression, which can manifest in physical illness. I don't know about you, but after the journey I experienced overcoming breast cancer, your girl is all over boundaries like peanut butter on jelly. That's why in this chapter you'll learn a simple boundary integration process you can adopt today. You'll also be introduced to the Offense Capacity Quotient, which will help you navigate difficult situations and conversations with confidence.

I'M NOT AVAILABLE

"I'm not available at 11 a.m., but I *am* available at 10 a.m., which is the time we agreed upon."

It was one of the hardest text messages I'd had to send in a long time, but I knew I needed to speak up; otherwise, I'd run the risk of repressing my emotions and developing deep-rooted resentment toward a friend I cared about. This wasn't the first time she had sent a last-minute request asking us to reschedule a call, but it was the first time I had the courage to say something. The previous half dozen or so times, I had made excuses and justifications for her. I told myself things like: *She's super busy. I don't have that much going on; it's really fine. I've canceled before; it's only fair that I show her grace. It's really not costing me anything to shift things around; that's what good friends do.* But on that day, I couldn't bring myself to make up any more excuses for her. Especially since when I saw her text message asking to reschedule, the first thing I did was roll my eyes and get angry. That's how I knew I needed to speak up. The seeds of resentment had already been planted.

If you're ever unsure about where you stand concerning a boundary you have with someone, pay attention to how you feel the moment a request comes up for that boundary to be bent or broken. Do you get angry? Do you feel sad, mad, hurt, or annoyed? Where does the emotion come up in your body? Pay attention to these small cues. *They matter!* It was the eye roll for me that let me know right then and there that if I didn't say something then, we were both in jeopardy of Rachel Rodriguez making an appearance—and *no one* wants to see Rachel Rodriguez come out of her face. (By the way, Rachel Rodriguez is my maiden name. She's also my less evolved alter ego. I do my absolute best to keep her and her petty ways at bay, but I'm not perfect, and every now and again she tries to claw her way into the limelight. *Not today, Satan, not today.*)

As I prepared myself to send an expanded, follow-up text message, I thought through some questions, much like those in the exercises you and I did earlier. *What's happening? What am I telling myself? What am I making it mean? What do I believe? What do I value? Who do I want to be in this moment?*

Permission Slip

I give myself permission to stop letting my belief in the goodness of others keep me from honoring my boundaries.

#PermissiontoOffend

At first I considered not sending the follow-up text message—the one in which I planned to say exactly what was on my mind and in my heart—because I knew part of what I was telling myself about her asking to reschedule was a story. I know my friend. I know her heart. I know her intentions. But isn't that part of the issue right there? The fact that we are willing to put our dreams, goals, wants, and desires on the back burner to accommodate someone else because our belief in their goodness is greater than our commitment to our legacy? No! I couldn't overlook it this time.

The truth is, although I *technically* didn't have anything on my schedule and could have easily moved the time of our call, I was in the middle of writing a book and refreshing my website and getting things aligned for the next iteration of who I am and the legacy I'm creating. It wasn't just rescheduling an hour; it was the mental and emotional energy of changing the direction of my day to prioritize someone else's business above my own. Nah. I wasn't available for that. So I began drafting the follow-up text message to share the stories I was telling myself about her constant rescheduling.

I knew I was risking hurting her feelings or possibly being the reason why she might then start telling her own stories because of *my* text message. (Remember the cycle we spoke about in chapter 1?) But I'm not responsible for anybody else's stories or feelings—*and neither are you!* I'm responsible for myself, for my own stories, and for making sure people know my standards. Honestly, I should have said something sooner.

I had to remind myself that we teach people how to treat us. If you don't set the standard in the moment, your boundaries will continue to be bent until they are broken. Had I chosen not to stand up for myself and honor my boundary, then I would have just been confirming for her and others: *It's okay to reschedule on Rachel at the last minute. It's okay to put her off until a more convenient time.* And it wasn't okay with me! This was an opportunity for me to be an Empathetic Offender and speak up for myself. So I did.

I explained that I knew I was telling myself a story and assigning meaning to her frequent rescheduling, but I needed to honor myself, my thoughts, and my feelings. I told her I knew she loved me, but her repeated cancellations weren't respectful of my time and I wanted to honor us both by calling it out. I ended the message with: "That being said, I'm not available at 11 a.m., but I *am* available at 10 a.m., which is the time we agreed upon. And I love you."

Yes, I was scared of all the what-ifs that might follow after hitting SEND. Let's be clear: I was extra scared and nervous to send that text. My heart was pounding. My hands were shaking ever so slightly. I felt all the things. Ultimately, I was more afraid of the long-term effects of *not* standing up for myself than the short-term discomfort I felt in the moment.

Think about all the times when you didn't speak up and how they've affected your life today.

Think about the times when you stayed quiet and let the other person gaslight you.

Think about the times when you backed down because you were afraid to upset someone.

Think about the times when you put your dreams and life on hold to help someone else fulfill theirs.

Practice saying, "I'm not available." Yes, there's a risk that some people will not be okay with you standing up for yourself, and yes, you might lose some people along the way. Dare I say it? You might even lose some family members. I'm reminded of the story of Lot and Abram (Gen. 13:1–18)—an uncle and nephew who had to separate to receive their blessings. But neither of them died before their time because of this separation, and neither will you! Remember, your brain is always working to ensure your survival, and anything that challenges the patterns and habits you've adopted is initially registered as a threat to your survival.* The antidote is to seek opportunities to honor your boundaries.

What if, by disconnecting from people who don't honor and

---

* "Why Change Is so Hard—and How to Deal with It," *Your Brain at Work*, NueroLeadership Institute, December 12, 2019, Institutehttps://neuroleadership.com /your-brain-at-work/growth-mindset-deal-with-change.

accept you as you desire, you open up the space for connection with people who will fully embrace and celebrate you just as you are, fully self-expressed? How awesome would that be?

What are the opportunities available to you and to the people you care about most when you make the change and choose yourself first?

BOUNDARY BULLIES

All right, so we've spent a good bit of time talking about how others try to cross our boundaries. But what about when the boundary bully is *you*? I know all about being my own boundary bully. Heck, I had to pop her one good just the other day.

I was registered to attend a virtual retreat, and although I had initially planned to rent a luxury hotel and sequester myself for the weekend, ultimately I chose to stay home because, well, your girl just didn't feel like packing. Anyhow, I told my family that even though I was staying home for the weekend, they were to "pretend Mama isn't here." "Don't ask me for anything, don't come knocking on my office door," I instructed my children. "If you need anything, go to Daddy. If there's an emergency, call 911 and then find Daddy. If you need a hug, hug Daddy. If you need toilet paper, scream for Dada." Then I went to my husband's office and gave him his own little speech. "This week-end I'm going to be part of a virtual retreat. *It will be like I'm not here.* You are going to have to feed yourself and make sure the kids and dog eat. Print any pages you need printed today because once my retreat begins I don't want you coming in and out of my office."

"But if you're not here, why can't I go into your office?" my clown husband shot back. I gave him *the look*, which warned him I wasn't playing games right now. "Don't use any of my stuff while I'm gone. My office is closed to you and everyone else. I'm not cooking. And I'm not precooking either, so make sure you have it figured out. Got it?"

It's taken me nearly thirteen years of marriage to get to the place where I have given myself permission to not be the one responsible for making every single arrangement while I'm away. Before this, I was the wife who would precook all the meals and put them in the freezer or make arrangements for meal deliveries and sleepovers so no one in my house was inconvenienced by my absence. Wish you could see me shaking my head as I reflect. It's one thing to do those things because they bring you joy and fulfillment. If they do, fantastic! Keep doing them. But I wasn't doing those things from a place of love, joy, and fulfillment. I was doing them out of fear and insecurity. I was afraid if I didn't do those things, then my family would feel neglected, my husband would think I was a bad wife, and my children would quite possibly go hungry.

My husband looked at me with a playful smile and said, "Got it, babe! Text you when I'm ready to eat and send the kids to you if they need anything." Then he kissed me on the lips and said, "Just kidding. I got it. The mama is gone. I'll order pizza and fried chicken for the kids."

"Great. Do whatever you need to do. I'm not here until Monday," I clapped back.

The first day of the retreat arrived and things were going great— until my own inner boundary bully popped up and told me to go give the kids a few hugs during the lunch break. Surely there's nothing wrong with a mom wanting to give her kids a few squeezes in between breaks, right? So off I went to each of their rooms and said, "Quick! Love and hugs before I go back in." My daughter Isabella's face lit up. "Mama! I thought you weren't here." Clearly someone other than me remembered what was supposed to be happening. "I'm not here. I'm just getting a hug and I'm out the door," I replied. I gave my other daughter, Valentina, a hug, and on the way back to my office I planted a big kiss on my husband's lips before heading in to enjoy the second half of the retreat. Honestly, those two hugs and that big kiss filled my heart with so much joy. It was a boundary well bent.

Boundary bully 1, Mama 0.

As day one of the retreat came to a close, I felt immense gratitude and fulfillment. I work from home, my husband is retired, and, thanks to the COVID pandemic, the kids were attending virtual school. We were *always* home, and this was the first time since the pandemic hit that I had been able to get any focused time to myself. How could that be? Simple. I had set firm boundaries and I had communicated how important this retreat was to me. I had enrolled them in my vision. Enrolling others in your vision is the key to setting and honoring your boundaries.

ALIGNMENT OPPORTUNITY

Let's practice setting a boundary and creating an enrollment process right now.

What's a boundary you've been wanting to enforce but that has been breeched by your inner boundary bully? (For example, "My desired boundary is three uninterrupted work hours," "My desired boundary is for my mom to respect my parenting choices.")

My desired boundary is:

_____

Now let's get clear on why this boundary matters to you. You'll need to be clear on this if you're going to get others around you enrolled in the vision.

This boundary is important to me because:

_____

Finally, I love and recommend journaling around how getting what I want affects the people I love. This step isn't 100 percent necessary, but it's really helpful, especially if you're someone who struggles with feeling guilty when setting boundaries.

This boundary benefits others besides me because:

_____

I had done a fantastic job of enrolling my family in my vision for the weekend. And then it happened . . .

My inner boundary bully showed up the next morning. *Wow! What a great night of sleep we got, and look how early we are. Maybe I should surprise the family with coffee for the hubby and donuts for the kids for breakfast. I could quickly get dressed, drive just down the street, and make it back in time before the retreat starts.* I thought about how good I would feel looking at their faces light up as I set the donuts on the table for them to indulge. That would make them so happy.

Screeeeeeeech. The sound of a record player needle scratching on vinyl went off in my mind. *What?! Noooooo!!! This is my weekend. I said I'm not here. Yes, I have the time, but if I do that, then I risk losing this precious time I have right now to center myself and prepare for day two of the retreat. No! I told them to pretend I wasn't here. I have to honor myself and my own boundaries. Otherwise, why did I waste my breath giving those instructions? Nope! Nope! Nope! They have plenty of food, and even if they don't, their dad can easily take them out for breakfast. This is my weekend and I get to have this time.* Kapow! Take that, boundary bully!

(P.S. Yes, I really do have these types of long conversations with myself.)

Boundary bully 1, Mama 1.

Instead of going to get breakfast for them, I poured myself a hot cup of tea, grabbed my journal, and enjoyed a powerful scripting session. Scripting sessions are what I do and teach when it comes to manifesting an upgraded life experience through journaling. It was such a joyful and fulfilling morning. And guess what? No one went hungry in my house, and from what I could see through the glass French doors of my office, everyone was happy, healthy, and thriving. But that was a close one!

Did you notice what happened? The moment I allowed my inner

boundary bully to bend my boundary, she tried the very next day to press a little further, and I'm certain if I had gotten those donuts that morning, my boundary would have been full-on broken by the final day of the retreat. Kids, dog, and husband would have been up my butt with demands and requests.

The question needs to be answered: *Who's really the boundary bully?* Is it you or someone else? Maybe it's you *and* someone else.

This makes me think of Sara, a woman who attended one of my live events. Sara reached out for a session to help her with some boundary issues she was having with a client. When she first started her business, she provided tech support, but as she began doing much of the work you and I have done together up to this point, she discovered she wanted to make the leap into coaching and consulting. The more Sara leaned into her values and owned her identity, the more she was able to see where she was being called. She began by coaching small groups and offering one-on-one strategic consultations, but she knew she was being called to speak at events and began by securing breakout sessions and virtual panel-speaking opportunities. Sara was beginning to find and use her voice. She was giving herself permission to offend! But she had this one last client who was still relying on her for technical support. Sara had already communicated to the client that she was making the transition to full-time speaking, coaching, and consulting and would no longer be available for technical services, but she said, "I don't want to leave you high and dry, so I'll stay on for the next thirty days to give you time to find a replacement and for me to do a proper training with that person." The client agreed.

Over the next thirty days, what Sara hoped would be a smooth transition turned into a nightmare. Her client would text with urgent demands, often during evening and weekend hours. She never began or ended her requests with any kind of pleasantries and would often snap rude, passive-aggressive comments Sara's way. Rather than stand up and activate her Empathetic Offender identity, Sara's Pleaser led the charge. She avoided confrontation, regularly broke her own client-contractor boundaries, and consistently battled feeling guilt and fear over what might happen if she stood up for herself.

As the end of their time working together approached, the client came back to Sara and said, "I just can't find anyone who can do all the things I need them to do. This is impossible. I need you to stay on longer. I'll pay you more."

One of the biggest challenges we'll face is that when we're on the precipice of change, others will want us to stay the same. As you can see from Sara's story, her client was so averse to Sara changing, she even tried bribing her with the promise of more money to stop her from moving on. This is a desperate manipulation tactic. Don't be deceived by a boundary bully. Often they will say and do whatever it takes to get their way. (This is true especially when you are your own boundary bully.)

Unfortunately, Sara stayed—not because of the money but because, as she put it, "I didn't want to leave the relationship on any kind of bad terms."

Permission Slip

I give myself permission to let some relationships end on "bad terms."

#PermissiontoOffend

How often have you stayed in a negative situation because you didn't want to end things like this?

Real talk: Relationships end poorly because of a lack of respect between one or more of the parties. If you are doing your part to show up in alignment with your values and your beliefs, then *oh well!* Give yourself permission to let some relationships end on "bad terms."

WHAT'S YOUR OFFENSE CAPACITY QUOTIENT?

How tolerant are you of the ideas, opinions, and judgments of other people? My personal goal is to get to a place in my life where I don't give a rat's tail about what anyone thinks, believes, feels, or says about me, my family, or my work—even if it's the person whose love and respect I crave the most. Scratch that—*especially* if it's someone whose love and respect I crave! Why? Because letting the ideas, opinions, and judgments of people, especially those I love and respect, can and have derailed me from pursuing my dreams. For example, I received a full scholarship to an art school, but my mom insisted I attend Penn State University and study business instead. Getting that full scholarship was a dream come true that could have made my financial future just a little more stable. Instead, I racked up more than $40,000 of student loan debt just so my mom could make good on a promise she'd made to my biological mother on her death bed. I remember my mom saying something to the effect of "If you don't graduate from college and get a good job, then they'll criticize me." The "they" she had been referring to were family members from my biological mother's side. If I had known then what I know now about stories, beliefs, identity, and how to navigate delicate conversations, I wouldn't have given up on my dreams of pursuing a career in the arts. I for damn sure wouldn't have taken on so many student loans. But *c'est la vie!* I'm at peace with how my life has turned out because I found a new dream and a career that I absolutely *love*, but for many years I held on to a lot of resentment and feelings of hopelessness as I tried to find my place in the world, absent of my childhood dreams. This is why I am in the continuous pursuit of not caring at all.

But what about those moments in life when caring about what others think *is* your business? For example, your boss's opinion of your job performance is your business. A client's satisfaction with your service *is* your business. Your partner's opinion of how you're showing up in the relationship is absolutely your business. So how do you stop caring so much about what others think while also still caring enough about your career, relationships, and all the things that matter to you most?

Well, it's simple. You raise your Offense Capacity Quotient, or OCQ. The higher your OCQ, the easier it is to move forward in faith and freedom. It's also a major opportunity for you to have meaningful dialogue, find connective tissue, and come together *even if* your beliefs are completely different from those of others around you.

Your OCQ is an indicator of how much offense you can tolerate receiving from others. It's a measure of your ability to remain firmly grounded in your identity regardless of someone else's thoughts, actions, words, or behaviors. Bottom line: the higher your OCQ, the more unbothered you are when someone says some off-the-wall BS. Your world isn't rocked; your foundation is solid and you can continue to move forward, unfazed.

Increasing your OCQ is important when it comes to embodying the identity of the Empathetic Offender and living a *Permission to Offend* lifestyle, because when you increase your capacity to be offended, you're able to listen and engage with people who might be saying or doing things that would otherwise enrage you and create discord.

I knew my own OCQ had increased when I shared a post on social media expressing my opinion on the interchangeability of the words "God" and "universe." Up until that point I would frequently say, "God, universe, source, whatever you want to call it." But in my heart, it felt like a betrayal of my beliefs and *my* God. So I did it: I wrote a post with *my* opinion and belief that God had created the universe and the two weren't interchangeable. I knew at least one person would be pissed and unfollow me, but it was a chance I had been willing to take to stand in my truth. Sure enough, about 500 people unfollowed me within the first hour. A few nasty comments trickled in, and then there was the one that really stood out among the rest. The woman wrote, "I just lost all respect I had for you. Unfollowing." To which I replied, "Thank you for sharing your thoughts."

In the past, I would have hidden under the covers, cried myself to sleep, and woken up to binge on whatever junk food I could find in the pantry. In the past, losing that many followers in such a short span would have been excruciating to my ego. Having practiced the work in this book over and over and over again prepared me for that afternoon. Instead of crying, binging, and contemplating my life choices, I chose to thank every single person who engaged with my post, whether negative or positive. I had several wonderful exchanges with people who didn't share my belief but respected my point of view. One woman wrote, "While my beliefs are different, I love this post. 💜 We all have different views, and to hate on each other for disagreeing on everything is insane. Thanks for sharing 💜 ."

I wrote back, "Thank you so much for joining in on the conversation and seeing my true intentions. I welcome you and I send you love and blessings 💜 ."

I would be lying if I said the comments and eventual loss of nearly a thousand followers in one day wasn't jarring at first. It absolutely was! After all, each follower is a *real* person. The loss felt like a thousand rejections, and it was something I had never experienced before. It reminded me that sharing your truth comes with consequences as well as opportunities. I think people forget about the opportunities because they're so afraid of the consequences. That day and for several days after, I continued to have positive dialogue with people

LOW OCQ THOUGHTS	HIGH OCQ THOUGHTS
Who do they think they are?	*I wonder what they mean?*
Idiots! I'm unfollowing!	*I'm going to stick around and see how this plays out OR I'm not aligned with these thoughts. I'll unfollow for now and check back in to see if this was just a human moment.*
I can't believe they did/said that!	*Oh, that's interesting. I would love to learn more to get the full scope.*
They're all going to laugh at me/ judge me.	*I won't be able to please everyone all the time. I'm going to go for it!*
If I do this I'm going to lose everything I love.	*If I don't do this, I might lose myself. I'm worthy to do what I'm being led to do. It's okay if others don't come with me.*

#PERMISSION TO OFFEND

who agreed and disagreed with my point of view. Each conversation helped me learn about myself as well as them.

This new way of being someone who can tolerate offense has allowed me to empathetically engage in deep, sometimes highly emotionally charged conversations. In some cases, these exchanges have helped my mindset shift, as I'm able to see and experience a new way of believing and being thanks to others sharing their philosophies. In some less fortunate moments, I've been led to walk away from friendships and relationships that were no longer serving me or them. The result, although painful in the moment, has been positive in the long run.

NOTE TO SELF

WHAT IS PAINFUL IN THE MOMENT HAS THE POTENTIAL TO BE POSITIVE IN THE LONG RUN. DON'T TRY TO BYPASS THE PAIN.

#PermissiontoOffend

None of these experiences ever would have happened if I hadn't increased my Offense Capacity Quotient. Sometimes when you increase your OCQ you discover you actually want the same thing as the person whose values and beliefs differ from your own—you're just expressing yourselves differently. This is particularly true for my mom and me. I've learned that if I'm not intentional about our dialogue, we easily find ourselves spinning around in circles, only to realize we're trying to get to the same place. Can you think of someone in your life you go through this with? You both want the same things, but your beliefs on how you're going to get there are so fundamentally different that if you're not intentionally and deliberately operating with a high Offense Capacity Quotient things might go off the rails?

When your OCQ is low, you run the risk of destroying or altogether losing opportunities, experiences, and relationships that could completely shift and transform your life and the lives of others. This is because you spend more time sitting in offense than working toward understanding.

Here are three simple steps to increasing your OCQ:

Get curious. *Ask clarifying questions. What did they mean? What do you mean? Are there any stories you're telling yourself? Are there any stories the other person is telling themself? Is there any common ground between you both? What if it's not personal? What if it is personal? What are you making it mean? What are they making it mean? Ask as many clarifying questions as you can to find a point of connection.*

Affirm your truth. *Continue to remind yourself of what you believe and value. When potentially "offensive" people or situations pop up, affirm your truth and take only the actions that align with your values and beliefs.*

Practice being "offended." *Start speaking, doing, and being exactly who you want to be. Pursue a passion, share a post with your beliefs, change your wardrobe—do the things you fear will offend others and practice responding with high OCQ thoughts.*

Curious to know your OCQ? Take the following quiz now.

1. You've spent weeks choosing the perfect paint color for your favorite room in your home. Once the walls are painted, you invite your friend over to check out your masterpiece. She walks in and the first thing she says is "Oh, it's cute, but did you mean to choose that paint finish?" You:

☐ immediately feel deflated and start second-guessing your choice.

☐ are low-key annoyed by the question but try to laugh it off and say, "Yes, why?"

☐ think nothing of it and say, "Yep! I love it."

2. You send your friend a text message and you don't get a response. A few days pass and you text again. Still no response. You:

☐ freak out and rack your brain, trying to figure out what you did wrong.

☐ wonder what's going on but decide you'll give them a few more days and maybe even give them a call to make sure nothing bad has happened.

☐ move on with your day and forget that you've even sent them a text message. After all, life is busy and you've got loads going on as well.

3. You're at a networking event and the conversation turns to politics or religion (you know, the "taboo" topics). The person to your left says something that completely goes against your personal beliefs. You:

☐ are immediately enraged. *Who the heck do they think they are?*

☐ feel jarred for a second and think, *Is this person for real?* Then you decide to keep quiet because you don't want any drama or conflict.

☐ think, *Oh, that's interesting. Let's see what this guy's story is,* and proceed to say out loud, "I disagree. Tell me more about why that's true for you."

4. You're having dinner out with your partner. Excitedly, you tell them about a new business idea. Without missing a beat, your partner looks you in the eye and says, "That'll never work." You:

☐ feel every range of emotion and can't decide whether to burst into tears or throw your glass of water right in their face. Through the rest of the meal you feel like a failure and contemplate all your life decisions.

☐ are taken aback and ask, "Why would you say that?" You feel a little hurt but think there might be an explanation.

☐ laugh and say, "Okay," but silently you start to visualize ten years in the future as you retell the story to an audience of thousands about that one time your partner told you it would never work but here you are with a multimillion-dollar business.

5. You're at a party with friends when someone comments on your outfit and says, "Those jeans are super cute, but it would look so much cuter with a camisole instead of that top you're wearing." You:

☐ are immediately embarrassed and feel self-conscious the rest of the night.

☐ start to take it personally but then remind yourself that everyone is entitled to an opinion, so instead you smile politely and say, "Oh? Yeah, maybe." Then you move on and mingle with others.

☐ say, "Thank you. These jeans are super cute, and I love this top. But thank you for your suggestion."

6. You start to speak up on social media about something you perceive to be a major injustice (think BLM, for/against abortion, healthcare, etc.). Comments begin to flood in, and almost everyone is completely against your position. You:

☐ go into panic mode. You start commenting with justifications to try to keep the peace. Ultimately, you end up deleting all your posts about the topic. You don't want to give in, but you're afraid to get #canceled.

☐ leave the post up but decide to go on a social media fast. The environment is getting toxic and you want nothing to do with it.

☐ respectfully and kindly reply to comments. You ask questions and seek to understand other viewpoints, even though you feel confident in your beliefs.

7. How often has this occurred: you've been told by others that they feel like they need to walk on eggshells around you *or* you've felt you need to walk on eggshells around others?

☐ more often than you'd like to admit.

☐ not often, but you may have heard/felt something like that once or twice.

☐ never. People know they are free to be exactly who they want to be around you, and you feel free to be exactly who you are around them.

8. Choose the most accurate description of yourself:

☐ I often have really strong, unintentional, emotional reactions—even to the most basic situations.

☐ For the most part I keep my cool, but if I feel really passionately about something, I tend to have strong reactions.

☐ I take my time to process and intentionally respond rather than react to circumstances and situations happening to and around me. It takes significant acts of God for me to have emotional outbursts.

Visit PermissiontoOffend.com/more to calculate your results. You'll also find tools and resources to help you practice increasing your score.

Note that your score will change depending on the day, and that's totally fine. When my client Elise took the quiz, she reported finding questions 3 and 6 very triggering. My friend Sharon took the quiz and said that as she was answering the questions, she realized that her answers would have been drastically different had she taken it two years ago. I share that with you to remind you that no matter where you currently stand in your OCQ, we are all works in progress. This continuous work is necessary because as you begin to set, define, and even reestablish boundaries, you're going to need a high OCQ to not feel bad about honoring those boundaries!

You're a dynamic human being, remember? Change is part of the journey. Everything in this book is an offering; nothing is a directive. Try it on for size, and if it doesn't fit into your values and beliefs, *let it go.*

OFFENSE IN ACTION

On June 6, 2020, half a million people gathered in various locations across the United States to protest in support of the Black Lives Matter movement.* More than a month of protests continued following that day. On January 6, 2021, six months later, the Capitol Building in Washington, DC, was stormed, and five people lost their lives. During both of these events, I found myself in an emotional struggle.

Let me be clear: I'm not here to promote any specific political party or religion or movement. I'm using this example to illustrate how raising my own Offense Capacity Quotient allowed me to see other points of view and for others to see my point of view as well. I had several conversations with people in which we were able to see and understand our differences, specifically where politics came into

---

* Larry Buchanan, "Black Lives Matter May Be the Largest Movement in U.S. History," *New York Times*, July 3, 2020, https://www.nytimes.com/interactive/2020/07/03/us/george-floyd-protests-crowd-size.html.

play. I also had conversations with people in which, although I could see and understand why their beliefs were logical to them, to me, they were completely irrational and illogical.

In those latter conversations, I was empowered to make confident decisions about how I was going to move forward with those individuals. Some friendships were demoted to acquaintanceships, some acquaintances were unfollowed, and some followers were blocked. Regardless of how little I agreed with them, I wasn't *offended*; rather, I was illuminated. I was grateful to see what certain people in my life believed. Choose illumination over offense and watch how your life changes.

On a positive note, there were a few encounters that I thought were going to go super south. You know the kind of conversation where the other person looks like they're going to pop off and then you might have to let them know you're not the one to mess around with? Yeah, there were some of those conversations. *But* because I was actively doing the work we've been doing together . . .

Examining my truth vs. my stories

Anchoring into my values and beliefs

Embodying my core identity of love

Holding my boundaries with love and empathy

. . . my feisty alter ego, Rachel Rodriguez, wasn't triggered or baited into engaging and driving the conversation off a cliff. Instead, I had some incredibly productive conversations, and thanks to some of my great friends and fierce offenders, I was able to step into a new layer of activism.

Prior to these encounters, I rarely, if ever, fully expressed my opinions on race or politics. I was afraid to offend or alienate people, especially my customer base. Heaven forbid my follower count dropped, because, as you know, you're only as powerful and important as the almighty follower count. (Please note the tone of sarcasm. You already know I've lost thousands of followers and here I still stand.) My point is that because I'm no longer easily offended, I rarely ever worry about offending others. And when others are showing up in their truth, I'm unbothered, unfazed, and unmoved from my truth. It's a whole new kind of freedom! Not just for me but for those around me too.

NOTE TO SELF

DON'T GET OFFENDED. GET CURIOUS.

#PermissiontoOffend

Here's another shoe to try on for size. *What if sometimes you need to be offended?*

My good friend Tiphani has helped me increase my Offense Capacity Quotient, not because she's been so kind and mindful with her words but rather the opposite. Listen! When I tell you Tiphani cares not who or how often she offends, it's an understatement. If anything, it's Tiphani who has helped me give myself permission to offend with the number of times she has never held back to tell me about myself and how displeasing my actions were to God. Ha! All jokes aside, the more I experience situations that, on the surface, seem offensive, the more I'm able to dig into who I want to be and how I want to add value to the world. That's the opportunity available to *you* as a result of leaning into offense.

HONOR YOUR BOUNDARIES

I wanted to introduce you to the OCQ before diving into this next piece because, as you define, redefine, set, and honor boundaries, you'll need to have an increased offense capacity to handle the potential outcome.

Remember Sara? She's the one who wanted to make a career switch from technical assistant to speaker and coach? I want to tell you what happened next with her and how honoring your boundaries sets you free. After Sara accepted her client's offer to stay on as a technical assistant in exchange for more money, she took the time to lay down some new work guidelines. She sent an email with a detailed list of things she could and could not do in this new contract, including not working weekends or answering emails past 6:00 p.m. Unfortunately, things went from bad to worse. During her client's next project launch, Sara found herself sinking in quicksand.

"Out of respect for the fact that we were in launch mode and I want my clients to have successful launches," she said during one of our coaching calls, "I was breaking my own damn rules and answering to her after hours, which makes it so damn difficult because I tried telling her that I really needed her to make an effort to communicate with me earlier in the day."

Note how asking someone to make an effort is not the same as telling someone to respect your boundary. Making an effort and doing are not the same thing. As you start to set boundaries, it's going to be necessary for you to pay attention to the words you use. They matter. Okay, back to Sara.

Long story short: during that session, Sara and I worked through many of the exercises you and I have worked through so far. We uncovered how some of Sara's stories and patterns from the past were showing up in her present and also how her identity as a loyal person was now hindering her freedom. Sara was so afraid of appearing disloyal, of having her client speak ill of her to others, and of disappointing her client that she confined herself to a self-imposed prison. Toward the end of our session, I asked, "How did you feel when you broke your own rules?"

She replied with a deep sigh, "Disappointed."

I could feel the weight of her emotions. My final question to her was: "Can you allow yourself the freedom to disappoint others so you stop disappointing yourself?"

NOTE TO SELF

ALLOW YOURSELF THE FREEDOM TO DISAPPOINT OTHERS SO YOU STOP DISAPPOINTING YOURSELF.

#PermissiontoOffend

"Yes. I have to," she said and immediately made the decision to give her notice. She drafted an email in that very moment, laying out exactly what she would and would not do in the next fourteen days. This time, she stuck with it. I'm pleased to share with you that today Sara's coaching and speaking business is thriving. She's making a six-figure income on her own terms, all because she was willing to do the work and give herself *permission to offend*.

PRINCIPLES OF WALKING IN OFFENSE

▶ Your brain initially registers change as a threat to survival.

▶ The antidote to the brain's threat perception of change is to seek the opportunity.

▶ Enrolling others in your vision is the key to setting and honoring your boundaries.

▶ It's okay to say, "I'm not available."

▶ A high Offense Capacity Quotient (OCQ) helps your relationships.

▶ Your OCQ increases as you begin to master the boundary integration steps in this book.

▶ A high OCQ helps you honor your boundaries, because you're not as concerned with the opinions of others and you're more likely to engage in difficult conversations with boundary bullies—including yourself.

▶ When you and others collectively increase your capacity to engage in conversations deemed "offensive," you are then able to find more common ground and create more global unification.

This chapter had a lot of great gems—if I say so myself, and I do. By the way, if it bothered you that I just gave myself a light pat on the back, maybe go back and read those OCQ parts again. If you didn't enjoy this chapter, that's fine, but should it bother you that I celebrated myself for writing it? Hmmmm . . . something to think about.

In all seriousness, I hope that, at the very least, you'll take away from this chapter the practice of enrolling others in your vision. This is key to ensuring your boundaries are honored. That one shift alone can make a big difference in your life. And then, if you want something extra—and God knows I love me some extra—practice putting yourself in a situation in which you can test your offense capacity. Listen to understand, bounce the other person's beliefs and values off your own, and look for some connective tissue. If you can't find any, then you've got some decisions to make, and we'll talk more about that later.

———— AFFIRMATION ————

THEIR TRUTH DOESN'T MAKE ME A LIAR. MY TRUTH DOESN'T MAKE THEM A LIAR. TWO TRUTHS CAN COEXIST IN THIS WORLD.

——————— #PermissiontoOffend ———————

Don't get tired on me now, friend. We're about to enter the judgment zone. Read on.

6

END THE VALIDATION ADDICTION

Whenever you receive validation, the reward center in your brain is activated and a quick hit of dopamine is released. Ahhh, dopamine. The feel-good drug humans can never seem to get enough of. It's why 66 percent of Americans check their phones up to 160 times per day![*] Each time you see a notification, your brain registers it as a reward and you get another quick hit. It's a momentary rush of pleasure, and each time it occurs, you unconsciously crave more of it.

One of the main reasons human beings want validation so often is because we've been raised to expect it. Think about how parents respond when a baby takes her first steps. Are they quiet and nonchalant or do they erupt in praise and celebration? As you grow through the school system, you are trained to seek validation through things like grades, awards ceremonies, and sports competitions. Controversially, participation trophies—awards given out to everyone who

---

[*] Gabrielle Pickard-Whitehead, "66% of Americans Check Phone 160 Times a Day, Here's How Your Business Can Benefit," Small Business Trends, March 3, 2020, https://smallbiztrends.com/2020/03/2020-mobile-phone-usage-statistics.html.

participated, not just the winners—have also played a role in this constant pursuit of validation. You've been conditioned to seek it. We all have! This kicks off a cycle.* More validation equals more dopamine equals desire for more validation for more dopamine. This is how the brain forms habits.

When I think about validation, I think about how badly we all want to be told we are good and *right*. By definition, "validation" is the action of checking or proving the validity or accuracy of something. The word that jumps out to me most in the definition is "proving." We want to *prove* to others, and by default ourselves, that whatever we have done or said is valid, accurate, and, at its core, *good enough*.

I know, I know—you already know you're good enough. Great! I know you're good enough too. Do you *believe* you're good enough? Are you that self-assured 24/7/365? If you're human, most likely not. If you're a unicorn, then maybe.

I'm not talking to the unicorns right now. I'm talking to the rest of us. Those of us who are brave enough to admit we don't have it all together all the time. Those of us who want to be told we've done a job well, that our dreams matter, that how we're showing up in the world is good and of value. I'm talking to those of us who, despite not wanting to, *do* care about what others think and say.

There's nothing intrinsically wrong with wanting validation from time to time, but as with everything in life, moderation is the key. No, validation isn't bad. It's the *addiction* to validation that poses the problem. It's the fact that you might be holding yourself back because you don't make any moves without first getting a stamp of approval from at least five other people or seeing a burning bush from God, the Most High.

---

* Mandar Natekar, "Seeking 'Validation' on Social Media and How It Is Killing Productivity at Work," LinkedIn, January 4, 2018, https://www.linkedin.com/pulse /seeking-validation-social-media-how-killing-work-mandar-natekar/.

As a lover of the Lord, I get it. I'm constantly in pursuit of God-approved goals. I've often told friends who share my beliefs, "Don't let the fear of human beings keep you from the favor of God." I want to cross them pearly gates of heaven and hear the words "Well done, good and faithful servant." Buttttttttt—and that's a big ol' but—it becomes a problem when I'm out here chasing approval from mortal human beings rather than staying in alignment with my beliefs and values (that is, my identity in my relationship with God). You know what I mean? You feelin' me?

Even if we don't share the same beliefs in makers and creators, can you and I agree on the fact that living in endless pursuit of validation from fallible humans is a waste of time, energy, and talent? Let's not waste our potential getting high on the approval and validation of others. Let's go ahead and set ourselves free. There's a better way.

> ## DON'T WASTE YOUR POTENTIAL GETTING HIGH ON VALIDATION.
>
> #PermissiontoOffend

GETTING SOBER

The key to kicking validation addiction is to replace validation with verification. You might be wondering, *Well, Rachel, isn't that trading one addiction for another?* No! It's not. Here's the difference: Validation is an emotional need. Verification is an analytical assessment.

Think about the last time you got into it with someone and you called your best friend to tell her what happened. Were you hoping your best friend would point out all your faults in the argument? Heck no! You called because you wanted your best friend to be Team You 100 percent! Tell me you know what I'm talking about.

Listen, when I'm feeling some type of way, the first person I call is my best friend, Melisa. And it goes a little something like this:

"Best friend!"

"Uh-oh, what's going on, girl?" (My best friend knows exactly what kind of mood I'm in by the tone of my voice.)

"Tell me why so-and-so just came all the way out of her face!" Major attitude is emanating from my end of the phone when I say someone came all the way out of their face. Basically, that's my way of saying I didn't like how someone spoke to me. Now, here's the part where you'll see just how much work my best friend and I have done in our relationship over the years.

Her response is always: "Hold up. Which best friend do you need me to be right now?" Ding! Ding! Ding! We've got the champion best friend in the house. She's approaching the conversation with her Empathetic Offender identity. Rather than diving into validation or criticism, she's operating from a place of heart-centered love and curiosity.

"Team Me, best friend! Team All. The. Way. *Me!* I don't care how right you might think they are, today we are Team *Me!*" is what I might say when I'm feeling particularly vulnerable and in need of validation and support. Remember, the desire for validation isn't necessarily bad. In fact, some studies have shown that receiving praise and validation can help the individual stay motivated, keep going, and do better in the future.* There's a time and a place.

Now, it's not always Team Me time. There are often moments when I'll say something like, "You can be *honest*, best friend. I'm available to be wrong."

---

* Aaron Stern, "Why Did Kids Start Getting Participation Trophies for Sports?," *Fatherly*, April 5, 2022, https://www.fatherly.com/play/participation-trophy/.

That's the critical first step to getting sober from your validation addiction. *You must be available to be wrong.* Remember, validation is what we seek when we have an emotional need to be right, approved of, and/or accepted.

Then I might give my best friend some metrics for the feedback I'm seeking. For example, I might say, "I'm available to be wrong, and specifically I want to know what you think I might have said or done that was out of order." This specificity creates more meaningful conversation and is also another boundary layer.

You know where this has really served me? In conversations with my mom. Because sometimes we turn to people looking for validation and we're met with straight-up tear-you-down, word-smack-you-in-the-face, soul-crushing criticism. Now, I know this has never been my mom's intention, but there have been many occasions in which I've turned to her for support and encouragement (aka validation) and she's come back to me with some crazy "That's what you get for . . ." non-helpful nonsense. Once I got sober from my validation addiction, I stopped putting myself in compromising and emotionally damaging situations. Instead, when I want comfort, support, and encouragement from my mom, I'm clear and direct. I'll say something like, "Mommy, I'm going to tell you something, and I don't want any feedback or advice. I just want you to encourage me and tell me it's going to be okay." Sometimes she might slip up and start to insert her opinion, at which time I remind her of my metrics. But overall, she's done a great job of honoring my boundaries and showing up for me the way I want and need.

That's the second step to overcoming validation addiction: *set metrics for verification.*

Don't complicate this. Simply take a moment to check in with yourself and decide what you want from the conversation:

What do I want and need?

Am I available to be wrong?

Am I looking for unconditional support or an honest opinion?

Am I seeking specific feedback?

What would I like to take away from this conversation/experience?

Like anything worth doing, this takes practice, and over time it becomes second nature.

The more you trust yourself, the less you'll seek validation and approval from others. You may have made some pretty big mistakes in your past—or maybe that's just me projecting my crazy past on you, but whatever. Let's wipe the slate clean and start fresh, here and now. You know how to trust yourself. Take on the identity of someone who can trust herself. You know how to do this too. Adopt the belief that you can trust yourself. Make trusting yourself part of your core values. Remember: Beliefs + Values = Identity.

Embodying the identity of someone who trusts herself will serve you very well, especially when it comes to making unpopular decisions. This next alignment opportunity will help you activate your self-trust. I challenge you to spend some good quality time with this one because it prepares you for the final step in your validation sobriety.

When you're aligned with your true identity, you're golden. When you start following the opinions and belief patterns of others and second-guessing yourself, things go awry. Anytime you start to feel uncertain, give this practice a try. You'll find that the more you practice, the more you'll start to be able to make bold decisions that—while others may not agree with them—will create radical transformation in your life.

ALIGNMENT OPPORTUNITY

Try this now.

Step 1. Make a list of three to ten mistakes or wrong choices you've made in the past. The timing of when these mistakes or poor choices occurred doesn't matter. Try not to overthink or judge the mistakes. Just dump them onto paper.

Step 2. Review each situation one by one, and think back to just before you made each mistake or wrong decision. Were there any red flags or inklings that you weren't on the right path? Was there a feeling or a nudge of discomfort that made you think, *Hmm, something feels off, but...* If so, put a little star next to that mistake or poor choice.

Step 3. Compare and contrast. How often did you ignore the small voice and little red flags waving in the distance? Even if you had only one or two instances when you heard the small voice or felt the nudge that something was off, that's proof that you *can* trust yourself. This is evidence that your innate sense of knowing is on point. You've got proof that if you actually lean into your values and beliefs, you can trust yourself. Your opportunity is to lean in more to those whispers and nudges.

DECISIONS BY COMMITTEE

For most of my life, I made the majority of my life decisions by committee. I got the term "decisions by committee" from my good friend Candice. It's her way of describing how we often turn to our friends, family, mentors, and even sometimes perfect strangers to help us make decisions.

By the time I was diagnosed with breast cancer, I had already been working on my validation sobriety for a few years. But when you're faced with a truly life-threatening situation, there's a propensity to want to revert to old survival patterns. Of course I wanted to be told I was going to be okay. I absolutely wanted validation and a promise that I was going to live. Basically, I wanted everything no one but God could give me. This realization forced me to lean in even more to my identity. *What do I value? What do I believe? How do I want to go on this journey?*

I knew for sure that I didn't want to go the conventional chemo-radiation path. And yet, hearing my oncology team give me all the grim stats and facts, I began to question my decision. *Am I doing the right thing? What if I'm wrong? What about my children?* These questions lingered as I went from appointment to appointment. Time was ticking and it felt like decisions needed to be made at lightning speed. Every day was critical. When your life is literally on the line, it's almost impossible not to want to consult with "the committee." After all, you're not the only one who will be affected. So I listened to what the doctors, my husband, my mom, my best friend, and even strangers had to say concerning the treatment options. Until it all came to a head one sunny afternoon.

"I'm not in denial!" I screamed into the phone as hot tears streamed down my face. "I know the diagnosis is cancer, but I will *never* accept it! Don't tell me how to feel about what's happening to *me!*" Rarely, if ever, in my thirty-nine years of life have I raised my voice to my mother. Remember, I had been raised to be seen not heard, to speak only when spoken to, and to respect my elders no matter what. Having worked for years to find my voice and integrate my identity, it was impossible for me to stay silent as she accused me of being in denial simply because I wanted to choose an alternate path for healing.

I had already decided and made it clear that, while I was willing to acknowledge the diagnosis, I would never accept the prognosis. I had shared with my family and the important people in our lives that

I didn't align with the very popular "F*ck cancer" mentality. Rather, my choice was to approach it with love, curiosity, and patience. Instead of fifty-two weeks of aggressive chemotherapy and radiation, I decided on lesser-known, somewhat controversial naturopathic modalities. I chose to thank the tumor for letting me know something was systemically wrong in my body. I did all kinds of "weird" things that most people, my mom included, didn't understand.

I wasn't surprised that people had a *lot* of opinions about the decisions I was making concerning my health. After all, going against popular or conventional opinion requires a high level of faith that, I personally believe, is lacking in many people these days. I was, however, surprised that my mom so desperately wanted me to take ownership of the disease. That's what set me off on that particular day. "Mommy, I've made my decision, and it's not up for debate or discussion. I know there's a cancerous tumor. I understand what that means. I'm not in denial. If I were in denial, I'd be doing nothing at all. That's not the case. I'm doing all the things. I'm taking radical measures. I'm just not doing all the things most people want me to do. I need you to get on board and support me with what I've already decided. I need you to be on my side. Can you do that?" My mom is amazing and, thankfully, not only did she say yes but she has been and continues to be on my side every single day, in every way.

Getting sober from validation addiction and forfeiting decisions by committee requires a tremendous amount of faith. It takes developing a deep sense of self-integrity and intimacy with your identity. It also demands you embody your Empathetic Offender identity and allow yourself permission to offend. I had to be willing to offend my mom by behaving in a way that was contrary to how she had raised me. I had to be willing to offend many family members and my medical team. It wasn't easy, but it was necessary. You'll see when you activate your Empathetic Offender and defend your truth: you get to experience a new level of freedom.

As a side note, friend, I have to confess. It was hard for me to write this part of my story. If I'm honest with us both, it's testing my faith and pushing me to the edges of discomfort. At the time I'm writing this, I'm only twenty months post-diagnosis. I'm nineteen and a quarter months free, clear, and with no evidence of disease. I still don't know if I made the "right" decision because the clock I'm up against continues to tick until I hit the five-year mark. Then another clock starts and the race to the ten-year mark begins. Then *maybe*, just *maybe*, according to "popular opinion," I get to say, "I did it! I beat cancer!" But there's no guarantee. At my scan a few weeks ago, the technician doing my mammogram told me she was twenty years free and clear, and in year

ALIGNMENT OPPORTUNITY

When I first began this work, I didn't want to admit I was the kind of person who not only craved but also *needed* validation in order to take action or continue moving forward. I thought I was stronger than that. I thought I knew better. Ha! Joke was on me. But then I did this exercise and my beautiful, hot-pink bubble burst. Let's do it together now:

Think back to the last time you asked someone for their opinion.

When that person gave you their opinion, and it wasn't as positive as you expected, how did you feel? Were you surprised, disappointed, sad? Maybe you felt irritated, misunderstood, confused?

If your emotions were in the vein of negativity, it's a good indication that you weren't seeking feedback or even encouragement. Nope, you were seeking validation.

If you could redo that experience, what are some metrics for verification you could have put in place instead of simply asking for feedback/opinions? (For example: ask the person to answer a specific question, create a specific time frame, or offer multiple-choice options.)

twenty-one found another lump. It's only by *faith* that I can share my story and say, "Yup! I did it. I made the right decision." Sometimes you'll have to make major decisions on faith alone. If you're operating in alignment with your truth, you won't be wrong—no matter how it all shakes out in the end. Disclaimer: I am *not* a medical doctor. I am *not* giving medical advice, nor am I claiming that what I did for my healing is a cure for cancer. Consult licensed professionals for health decisions. The end.

The validation and certainty we crave is an illusion. It serves no one to chase after that which does not exist. Validation itself is an illusion. We want to be right, and surely there will be at least one person on a planet full of billions who will say we're wrong. Forget validation. Go for verification.

No one is saying that wanting to be validated is *wrong*. Remember, it only means whatever you make it mean. Seeking validation only becomes problematic when you stop trusting yourself (or in my case, when I stop trusting God) and continue to rely on the approval and opinions of others over your own knowing. Validation is what you seek when you want to stay in your comfort zone. Verification is what you establish when you're ready to go to your next level.

JUDGE ME, JUDGE ME, SAY THAT YOU LOVE ME

We've established that this is a safe space. I'm not going to judge you. Well, actually, I already have. I had to. In order to write a book that I believed would help transform lives, I had to make several assumptions and judgments about who you are, what stage of life you're at, and what some of your most pressing issues might be that have been holding you back from living in truth, faith, and freedom.

You've likely already made several judgments about me and/or this book too. That's okay. Judge away, friend. Again, take whatever you need from this book, embrace the nuggets that align with your values and beliefs, and ditch the rest. No love will be lost on my end. I promise. The reality is, we're all judging one another in some way, shape, or form. It's going to continue to happen for as long as we continue to show up in the world. Judgment happens. We covered this already: most thoughts are automatic.

In fact, researchers have found that specific areas of the amygdala are activated based on judgments of trustworthiness and untrust-worthiness. This, the researchers concluded, is evidence that our brains make judgments of people before we even process who they are or what they look like.*

If you've been feeling guilty about being judgmental, you can relax. Your brain is doing what it's been programmed to do. I mean, seriously, when was the last time you sat and thought, *Let me sit here, pick this person apart, and judge her for the next ten to fifteen minutes,* with intentional malice? I'm sure if you're a kind, loving, caring person the answer is *never.* If you're an a-hole, then maybe *often?* But seriously, it almost never happens that way. The judgment just happens, and I for one welcome it. Because to me, the meaning I have assigned to judgment from others is this:

If you're judging me, then I've got your attention. This is my chance! You see me. You hear me. You're paying attention to me, in one way or another, and that's an opportunity for me to walk in my calling. Pay attention to what I have to say and what I'm trying to do in this world because you might be the person to help me advance this movement and I might be the one to help you transform your life. Either way, if you're judging me, then we have an opportunity to be of service to each other. Moreover, this reciprocal service isn't

---

* Alexandra Sifferlin, "Our Brains Immediately Judge People," *TIME*, August 6, 2014, https://time.com/3083667/brain-trustworthiness/.

simply reduced to what we can do for each other—it's also about how we each can grow with each other. The power of judgment is breathtaking, especially when we observe and process the awareness of our judgment together.

ALIGNMENT OPPORTUNITY

Use these journal prompts to get in touch with what's holding you back.

Where have I not been showing up for fear of judgment?

Whose judgment do I fear the most?

What's the worst thing I fear will happen?

How will my life change—what will I lose—if my worst fears come true?

What's the best thing that can happen as a result of my showing up in one area of my life today?

Bonus: Take bold action and show up/speak up/stand up in one area where you've been hiding. Allow yourself to be seen and heard. The judgment, if any, will simply be an acknowledgment that people are paying attention. Now you've got the power.

Can you embrace it? Can you allow yourself to be bruised but not broken by judgment from others? Even beyond that, can you allow yourself to be seen, praised, and celebrated for having shown up in the first place and standing up for your truth? Or do you habitually find yourself saying, "Don't judge me"? Have you been so concerned with someone else's judgment that you have to ask their permission to not be judged? What in the world? Who started that trend, and can we end it here, now, today, once and for all? I get it. I've been guilty of saying it too. Especially on mornings when I've logged on to social media and my messy kitchen can be seen in the background. "Don't judge me. My kitchen is a mess." "Don't judge me. I haven't put on my makeup." "Don't judge me." Get over it already. Let them judge. The only way to avoid judgment is to stay hidden. Even then, you might be judged for not showing up.

Permission Slip

I give myself permission to stop saying, "Don't judge me."

#PermissiontoOffend

The beautiful thing about moving from validation to verification is that you give yourself permission to set the standard. Verification is about giving yourself permission to be wrong while also asking for feedback that fits parameters and criteria set by you. It's your own personal measure, not based on what someone else wants to impose upon you. These metrics should align with your values, beliefs, and desired outcomes. When you give yourself permission to do this, you stop trying to measure up to the standards of others and you embrace setting the standards yourself. The need and desire to be validated creates a wedge between you and your ability to live in truth, faith, and freedom. Verification paves the path to freedom.

BRUISED, NOT BROKEN

A comedian was asked to join a conference call to discuss the potential of joining a few other comedians on tour. She joined the meeting early, unbeknownst to the other women on the line, and as she sat there on mute, she heard them take turns talking about her. It wasn't the good talk either. No, their venomous words were judgments about her appearance, comedic skill, and potential contribution—or lack thereof—to their tour. Can you imagine silently sitting on the other end of the phone, listening to people you respect, admire, and are excited to work with as they talk smack about you and question your talent, value, and worthiness? *¡Ay, señor, no!* Devastating, I'm sure! That's exactly what was going on. Can you guess what the woman listening in on this conversation did next?

Nothing.

Not a damn thing. She kept her phone on mute, kept her mouth shut, and took notes.

I don't know about you, but I don't think I would have been able to sit there quietly with my mouth shut. Nope. Not this girl. Well, not Rachel Rodriguez. Maybe Rachel Luna *might* have—and that's a big might—depending on who was on that call. Because giving yourself permission to offend isn't about burning bridges and alienating; it's about standing up when it matters most. As I listened to this woman tell her story, I wondered if it was wisdom or worry that kept her quiet.

NOTE TO SELF

LET WISDOM, NOT WORRY, KEEP YOU SILENT.

#PermissiontoOffend

Several years later, as the woman shared her story on national television, she said, "I was so shocked and hurt that I could not un-mute my phone and go, 'Hey, b*tch, I hear you!' . . . I stayed for all of the call with my phone on mute. But I thought, *Take notes. Listen.*

Because rarely would we hear someone talking about us and saying what they truly feel about us. . . . After I listened to this . . . I was bruised, but I was not broken."

As the TV segment drew to a close, she turned to the audience and relayed how she had never said anything to the other women and had, in fact, worked with each of them individually on other projects. She said, "Instead of being angry and vengeful, I decided to take the truth of what they were saying—and their right to have an opinion—and make myself an even better person. . . . I'm right where I belong." The audience erupted in loud applause and celebration.

That woman was Sheryl Underwood. She was telling her story on the very popular nationally syndicated US television show *The Talk*, which she has been a cohost on for more than a decade. Sheryl's final words concerning the situation were these: "I thank them for the blessing of telling me something that maybe I needed to hear because this is where I needed to get to and they helped me get here."[*]

Sheryl was able to leverage a very painful moment of judgment to help get her closer to her legacy. What past judgment can you learn from and leverage? Like Sheryl, are you willing to let the bruising of judgment help you develop into who you were always meant to be?

I KNOW YOU ARE, BUT WHAT AM I?

I'd be remiss if we moved on and I didn't share just one more point concerning judgment. Over the years, I've heard many stories from women who have struggled tremendously with procrastination. They were consistently inconsistent and their fear of judgment ran deep. Here comes the plot twist: These women weren't afraid of random

---

[*] Trina Divaa, "Sheryl Underwood Bruised But Not Broken @TrinaDiva," YouTube video, 5:33, posted October 3, 2014, https://www.youtube.com/watch?v=ahYe3p_yvKA.

judgment. Nope. These homegirls were terrified of being judged as harshly as they had judged themselves and others. Ooooh. Did you feel that?

As I dug into their experiences and stories, I was able to identify that many of the women who feared the judgment of others were holding on to a lot of guilt and shame for having been judgmental themselves. One woman in particular, Sharece, felt this way when it came to leaving her marriage. Having been brought up in a devout Christian home, she was raised to believe divorce was unacceptable, and let's not even talk about what others would say if she were to break up her home and become a single mother.

Additionally, it was living according to the values and beliefs that had been imposed on her as a child that kept her suffering silently in her marriage. Beliefs such as *Don't speak up* suffocated her when her husband impulsively bought himself a Mercedes-Benz without discussing it with her. This purchase put their finances at risk and caused their rent to be late on multiple occasions. When she needed help around the house after their son was born, all she could hear was the echo of her mother's voice saying, *Don't upset your husband; his job is stressful enough.* Perhaps the most damaging narrative of all was the reminder she gave herself: *Men cheat; just look the other way,* which echoed in her mind when she found a letter from her husband to another woman in which he declared the woman was his "soul mate." Sharece's true identity was mangled. Each day, rather than "offend" or "rock the boat," she bounced between the Pleaser and Critic identities, wearing whichever helped her survive the day.

She often thought about the many harsh judgments and comments she herself had made about other divorcees and single moms. "All the sh*t I've said about people who get divorced—and single moms?" she told me in a questioning tone. "What am *I* gonna look like?" These concerns of being judged as harshly as she had judged others caused Sharece to stay unhappily married for many years.

Ultimately, it wasn't Sharece who asked for the divorce. In the end, it was her husband who chose to dissolve the union. Today, Sharece is learning to adjust to her new role as a single mom, and she's actively working on redefining her true identity.

Hearing Sharece's story, can you relate? Or maybe you can find some connective tissue in Kelly's story.

Kelly is a very successful coach who works with high-performing female executives. When I asked her if she had ever held herself back because she was afraid of being judged as harshly as she had judged others, she quickly recalled one week in particular. "When my podcast hit one hundred episodes, I got featured in a magazine and all these great things were happening for me. I asked myself, *Should I even post that?* Because I remembered all the times in the past when I would eye-roll, watching other women celebrate their successes. I would make side comments like, *Oh, you're talking about how much money you make and how great you are, again?* It was really just all the self-comparison stuff. So when I had that week where all these great things were happening to me, I was hesitant to post all my wins. I thought, *Am I celebrating too much? What are people going to think? Are they going to roll their eyes at me the way I've rolled my eyes at other women?*"

I don't know about you, but I can relate to both Sharece and Kelly. Especially the part where Sharece said, "What am *I* gonna look like?" It's like the taunting game my friends and I played as children: "I know you are, but what am I?" I know how being caught in a moment of low self-esteem and comparison has led me to unfairly judge other women in the past. This caused me to question my own shine-worthy moments. Quite frankly, these experiences kept me living small when I knew God had created me to live big.

Your turn. Think of a time when you've held a judgment against someone, only to find yourself in a similar situation. Can you see how that might hold you back from moving forward? If so, not to worry. Here are three journal prompts to help you process and move forward:

Am I willing to forgive myself for judging people?

What's the most empathetic position I can take toward them and myself?

How does holding on to this help or hinder my ability to live freely?

My favorite prompt is the second one because empathy is such a wonderful unifier. But all three prompts bring value to the table, so try them out and help set yourself free.

──────AFFIRMATION──────────────────

I SEEK VERIFICATION, NOT VALIDATION. WHEN OTHERS JUDGE ME, IT'S EVIDENCE I'VE BEEN SEEN AND HEARD.

──────────────────── #PermissiontoOffend ──────

Use this affirmation to remind yourself to seek verification, not validation, and embrace the judgments of others.

PRINCIPLES FOR ENDING THE VALIDATION ADDICTION

▶ Most judgment is automatic and unintentional.
▶ When others judge you, it's an indication that you have their attention.
▶ The only way to possibly avoid judgment is to stay hidden, although you might then be judged for not showing up.

❯ Let wisdom, not worry, be the thing that keeps you quiet.

❯ The pursuit *of* validation creates the desire *for* validation.

❯ The path to freedom is marked by verification, not validation.

❯ Seek verification over validation.

Have you ever found yourself feeling super proud of a really good friend or maybe even someone you've never met personally but follow and admire? That's how I feel right now, knowing that you've completed this chapter. Working through judgment and validation requires a lot of honest, come-to-Jesus (or whomever you serve) moments. It also requires you to practice, which will ultimately lead to your mastery. The more you forgive yourself for your automatic judgment of others and allow yourself to be judged as well, the easier it will be. As you start creating verification metrics rather than seeking validation, you'll for sure notice that not only does your confidence increase but so will your resilience. Ultimately, your ability to say and do whatever you want without losing your self-integrity becomes automatic and not an afterthought.

Guess what else? Struggle doesn't have to accompany you for the rest of the journey. Let's explore that some more, right now.

7

RISK YOUR REPUTATION

I felt like the mother of all mom sheroes when my daughter looked up at me with adoring eyes and said, "Wow, Mama! That was awesome. You were so brave, and now look! We can make lemonade and maybe even sell it to the neighbors."

I'm not sure if mother of all mom sheroes is really a thing, but considering that I had previously suffered from undiagnosed postpartum depression and struggled to bond with both of my daughters for the first several *years* of each of their lives, this momentary pleasure of bonding and connection felt indescribable. Even as I recount the memory, I can still remember how her eyes lit up and how excited she was. Truly, gratitude abounds.

Having been told as a teenager I would most likely not be able to have children, suffering three miscarriages (one in between our two daughters), and then finally having my daughters and not being able to bond with them, it felt like my entire journey to motherhood had been one betrayal after another. So this moment—the moment when my eldest daughter beamed with pride at my bravery—it was special.

We had been on our daily walk around the neighborhood—a practice I adopted after healing from breast cancer. I learned that walking thirty minutes per day at any pace reduces the risk of breast cancer recurrence by up to 50 percent. Needless to say, I was sold! So on this day, as Isabella and I turned onto the main road, I said, "Look, Bella, there's a tree up ahead that has oranges, and every time I pass by I want to reach out and grab one."

"Do it, Mommy! Grab one." My girl is a brave one. She's always asking to go on adventures and discover new wonders.

"No way, lady! That's stealing. But, man, I wish I were a thief right now," I replied with a little chuckle. "I always want to ring the doorbell and ask them if I can have one, but . . ." My voice drifted off. We were getting closer to the house, and I could feel something rise up in me. This was an important moment—I could feel it. How I chose to handle my own desires would teach my daughter how to manage hers. Oh, the pressure!

"Maybe I should ask today?" I said to Isabella.

"Yeah, Mama, ask! You can do it," Isabella cheered me on.

"Well, let's do it on the return because we still have a ways to go on our loop; this way our hands will be free while we walk," I said. We continued walking and talking about random things, but I hadn't forgotten about my orange.

Growing up in New York City, I had never even seen real orange trees until we moved to Florida, and even then, I had never experienced the joy of tasting the sweet, tangy juice of the fruit freshly plucked from its branch. I'd gone apple picking, pumpkin picking, and even strawberry picking when we lived in Germany, so I knew the satisfaction of being able to reach out, touch, and taste the fruits of nature while actually *being* in nature. Something about it just makes me feel so connected to God and all of creation. There's something about it that makes me feel part of the circle of life. It's the freedom of knowing God always provides.

As I allowed my mind to wander, only half listening to Isabella's stories, we made the turn back, and I could see the tree up ahead.

This was it. The moment of truth was upon me. This was my moment to walk my talk. Except, *I was terrified.*

"Okay, Bella, this is it. We're coming up on the house. Yikes! Why am I so scared?" I said out loud. While I can't imagine I'll ever write a book on parenting—trust me, that's not my zone of genius— one thing I've learned is the importance of being honest with my children about my feelings. By showing my daughters that it's okay to be scared, I'm giving them permission to sit with those feelings as well. This has allowed us many opportunities to share a dialogue about their feelings, as well as for me to help them navigate tough moments.

"You can do it, Mama!" Bella repeated.

"But why am I scared?" I asked. Going into a monologue of rhetorical questions, I began thinking out loud. "I'm scared because what if they think I'm crazy? I'm scared because what if they say no? This is silly. So what? Who cares if they think I'm crazy? *I* care, because what if they end up putting a special notice in the community newsletter blast: 'Attention all Puerto Ricans from New York City, please stop knocking on neighbors' doors asking for oranges. Grow your own or go to Publix and buy them.' Ay, no!"

Not giving Isabella a chance to get a word in edgewise, I continued on:

"I know these thoughts are silly, Bella, but I want you to see how I process my thoughts when I'm scared. I want you to see how I validate or disprove my own thoughts and stories.

"The bottom line is that, yes, I'm scared the neighbors will think and do and say all those things, but at the end of the day, it comes down to the fact that I'm scared of being rejected, and I'm afraid *you* watching me get rejected will make you not want to take risks yourself. And all of those reasons are *exactly* why I'm going to knock on the door right now. Say a prayer for me, baby girl."

"You got this, Mommy!" She clapped and smiled.

We walked up to the door, and I pushed the little black button to ring the bell. My heart was beating out of my chest. You might be thinking, *Really? All that over an orange?* Yes! Really. *All* that over an orange. Your girl was scared!

Did I mention that I live in an "established" gated community? And by "established," I mean older white people. Most of my neighbors are retired seniors who spend a lot of time tattling on one another on our community group page. These people here do not mess around. One time the very back part of our yard had moss growing on it, which I thought looked nice, but it turned out to be "weeds." Well, someone complained and we got fined! For moss!!! You couldn't even see it from the road. Someone had to be really all the way up on our lawn to see it. Seriously, these people just have way too much time.

After waiting for what seemed like an eternity, but was really probably just thirty-four seconds, a man in what looked to be about his seventies answered the door. His facial expression confirmed my every fear. *Uh-oh. This dude is not going to be available for me and my orange-picking pleas.* Towering over my four-foot, eleven-and-a-half-inch frame, he said, "Yes?"

"Hi?" I said hesitantly. "I'm so sorry to bother you, but I walk by your house every day, and I always notice your orange tree . . ."

His face wasn't getting any kinder. He looked a combination of confused and annoyed.

"And I was just wondering . . . I've never had an orange from the tree before. Could I take one?" There! I did it.

Suddenly his face softened, and he smiled and said, "I'll do you one better. Take three."

What???? He said yes! He said take three! Not one, but THREE! Inside I was jumping up and down like a little kid. "Really? Thank you so much! I really appreciate it."

With that, the gentleman smiled and closed the door.

"Bella, did you see that?! He said take three! You see, baby girl, all ya gotta do is risk your reputation and ask!" I said. And then my heart stopped.

"Excuse me!" An older woman came out the front door.

Uh-oh.

"He doesn't know what I plant or what I do out here," she yelled over at us.

Oh no. This was it. She was going to tell me we couldn't take the oranges. Maybe these were prize-winning oranges or she was part of some garden club or maybe, like me, she was on the Gerson Therapy and needed every last orange for her morning juices. Whatever it was, I braced for impact.

"Those aren't oranges," she said. "You can take as many as you want, but those are Meyer lemons, and I wanted to make sure you knew before you bit into one of them and got something you weren't expecting."

Phew! That was close.

My heart rate returned to normal as the kind woman proceeded to walk us through her property, pointing out other fruit trees. Then, holding out a plastic shopping bag, she said, "Here you go. Take as many as you like. I can't keep up with them."

I reached out and grabbed the bag, thanking the woman for her generosity.

As we pulled lemons off the tree together, that's when Isabella looked over at me and said, "Wow, Mama! That was awesome. You were so brave, and now look! We can make lemonade and maybe even sell it to the neighbors." Like her mama, my baby is a natural-born entrepreneur, always looking for a way to create and sell something.

This sweet, special memory was only possible because even in the face of my fear, I chose to risk my reputation among my neighbors. I turned a key, and not only did I set myself free but I also showed

Isabella that she too could risk her reputation and find freedom. Or at the very least Meyer lemons.

That afternoon Isabella, my youngest daughter Valentina, and I all made Meyer lemonade together, and it was a beautiful afternoon of bonding, connecting, experiencing Meyer lemonade together for the first time while making sweet memories.

I gave myself permission.

I answered the call.

I practiced obedience.

I risked my reputation.

I turned the key.

I gave my girls hope.

I found freedom.

TURNING THE KEYS TO FREEDOM

Friend, we're at the part of the book where you can't un-know what we've made known together. Granted, you could totally go back to the work we did in chapter 1 and decide that none of what we've covered is of service to you. But even then, you'd know that while you can control the narrative in your own mind, you can't (nor should you even try to) control the narrative others have as they experience you.

You get to draw a line in the sand right here and now. Decide who you want to be, what you're going to do, and what you want to have as a result of honoring your truth and identity. As needed, you'll embody your Empathetic Offender identity, and with that comes one of the toughest decisions you'll have to make: *Are you willing to risk your reputation?* More specifically, are you willing to risk the reputation you had as the former version of yourself? That's what is required in order to step into this new, next-level iteration of who you really are.

It's a scary leap for many, but you're ready for a quantum leap. You were not created to blend in. You have been called to come out of hiding by virtue of the fact that you are reading this book and have made it this far.

Permission Slip

I give myself permission to risk my reputation.

#PermissiontoOffend

Blame it on your upbringing, blame it on your trauma, blame your children, your partner, your boss, your government, society, whoever, but deep down you know that every time you've been led where you dream of going, *you* are the one who has held yourself back. Notwithstanding the certain exceptions to every generalization, for the most part it's been *you* who has held the ultimate permission slip in your very own hands. You've been so scared to ruin your reputation that you've allowed your permission slip to get crumpled and rumpled beyond recognition. Heck, you might be in a position where you can't even remember what you wanted permission to do in the first place.

But it's okay! Slowly take a deep breath and when you can't fill your lungs anymore, hold it for four seconds. One . . . two . . . three . . . four. Exhale. Again: Inhale for a count of four. One . . . two . . . three . . . four. Hold it. One . . . two . . . three . . . four. Exhale and *release*. Let all the guilt, shame, blame, and resentment blow away. Fear may be present, but you have the power to move with or without it. What if instead of trying to completely eliminate fear you choose to recognize it as a protective parent in your life? What if fear is just a helicopter parent who wants nothing more than to hover over you and make sure you stay safe and protected for the rest of your life, by any means necessary? It's there. It's not going away. Handle your fear like one might handle an overbearing parent. Be clear in your intention. Understand fear's motives. Set boundaries. Follow all the steps we covered in chapter 5 and keep it moving! You can release fear's grip on you. It doesn't have to cut off the flow of your lifeblood.

While you're releasing yourself from fear's grip, how about also releasing your grip on old permission slips you've been hoping to one day gain the courage to use? You don't need them anymore. Today you're going to write a new kind of permission slip. It's the one that allows you to risk your reputation with the full faith and trust that, in doing so, not only will you be honoring your identity and entering into your purpose but also you'll be changing the lives of the people around you—the people you care about most as well as the people you haven't even encountered yet. Can you allow yourself to feel that for a moment? Try it. Close your eyes and spend just a minute or two breathing and thinking about these questions:

> *What if this is my last call—am I ready to leave this world knowing I didn't answer it?*
>
> *Do I want my legacy to be that of someone who was timid and shy, or do I want to be remembered as someone who was willing to risk her reputation for the sake of making a difference?*
>
> *Am I ready to run with the permission I've been asking for?*

Every time I force myself—yes, *force* myself (it's not always easy for me to intimately connect to my soul)—to answer these questions, I'm immediately filled with so much energy and conviction. Especially that last question. I'm not immune to any of this work. I want permission too. At my soul level, I too crave validation. I want confirmation that I'm on the right path. But if you and I never even allow ourselves to walk the path, how will we know? This is why you have to create your own verification metrics. This is why you have to give yourself permission to *write* your permission slips. This is why you must be willing to risk your reputation. So that when you start walking on the unpaved road and people start calling you everything but your chosen name, you can do so in full faith and freedom. And I promise you: *there is freedom on that path!*

This I know for sure: others will talk about you regardless. They will continue to judge your every move, even when you do exactly what they think you should be doing. You might find that this works for you in the short-term, but you will never find freedom. You will have confined yourself to a white-collar prison, the kind where inmates are offered workout classes, cable TV, and email access. A prison where the inmates manage to create community and connection. This provides some semblance of happiness and normalcy but never offers true fulfillment or freedom.

Imagine this: You hold several keys in your hands. These keys are all your great ideas, your goals, your action items—all the things you said you would do one day. Among these keys there's at least one that will open your prison door and set you free. But in order to find "the one," you first have to use each individual key in front of all the other inmates, none of whom believe there's any way out. With each key you try to turn, your "street cred on the block"—aka your reputation—diminishes. But you have *faith*. Something in you just *knows* there's a key that will not only let you out but also release several of your fellow inmates. This key, too, will provide hope for the others who are not yet ready to escape with you.

That's the permission and power you hold in your hands right at this very moment. All it takes is your willingness to risk your reputation.

Why do you stay in prison when the door is wide open?

—RUMI, "A COMMUNITY OF THE SPIRIT"

IN ORDER TO RISK, YOU MUST RELEASE

You will consistently get more of what you want after you learn how to release your emotional attachments to the outcome. As Isabella and I doubled back and I found myself confronting the Meyer lemon (not orange) tree, all my fears were tied to the outcome, not to the ask itself. Often we're afraid not of the doing but of what follows what we do.

What's going to happen when all my dreams come true?

Which of my relatives is going to ask for money?

Which friend is going to leave?

Which family member is going to think I'm bougie?

These are just some of the fears I've heard in the last decade. It's almost as if there's a story playing on repeat that says, *If I get what I want, I'll lose what I have.*

Part of me wants to tell you that's not true. "*Of course* you won't lose what you have once you get what you want." But I can't make that guarantee. However, I can say with 100 percent certainty that it doesn't *have* to be true. Sometimes getting what you want *does* require letting something go, but not because you don't love or care about those things; rather, it's because those things (or people) can't accompany you where you're going.

Some people just aren't ready. And the last thing you need is their negative influence and energy holding you down while you're rising up.

THE ALL OUTCOMES MATRIX

We were flying back from an incredible spring-break trip in Florida, when on our descent into JFK Airport in New York, our plane dropped, what I now guess to have been about 1,000 feet but what felt like 10,000 at the time. As the plane dipped, I looked out the window and saw the water rising to meet the wing of the plane. I was terrified. Others in the plane screamed out loud. This wasn't a "Rachel is being dramatic" situation, although I have certainly been guilty of many of those in the past. No, this was a real "Holy shizz" moment. To my right, a young boy about six years old said, "Wheeeee. This is fun, Mom," while other passengers gripped their armrests and prayed out loud. The plane continued to bounce up and down until we finally touched the runway. Shortly after landing, the pilot got on the intercom system and announced, "Sorry about that, folks. We're being held on the tarmac to fill out a report of what just happened. We flew into the jet wash of a jumbo jet, and that's what gave us that little jolt. We'll be on the ground for a bit, but we'll do our best to get you off the plane as soon as possible."

Other passengers had already calmed down once we landed, but not me. Since I was still crying loudly, the flight attendant came over and asked me if I was traveling alone or if there was anyone with me. "My friends are in the back," I said in between sobs. "Can I go be with them?" The friendly attendant helped me out of my seat and walked me toward my friends Geuris and Oso. When I saw the guys, I erupted in a deeper sob. Geuris quickly stood up, looking somewhat confused. "*¿Qué te pasa?*" he asked. ("What's wrong?") I don't remember what I said, but I do remember clinging on to him as if my life were still in danger. "You're going to need to sit down, honey. You can't stand in the aisles." The flight attendant motioned us toward the row. "*Ven, siéntate,*" Geuris said as he sat down and pulled me onto his lap. I felt foolish for crying so hard; I *knew* we had landed and I was safe, but I couldn't help but recall the image in my mind of the wing of the plane so frighteningly close to the water. Still crying, I said in Spanish, "I want to get off the plane, please. I want to get off the plane. We almost died. We almost died."

Geuris, God bless him, stroked my back and affirmed me. "*Ya aterrizamos, Raquel, cálmate.*" ("We've already landed, Rachel. Calm down.") And he was right. I was safe. I did my best to calm down, and a short while later we were allowed to safely disembark the plane. I took the train to my mom's house. Safe and sound. But that one experience was so traumatic that for *years* I struggled with an intense fear of flying. It got so bad that I would have nightmares days before getting on a plane. I couldn't fly without Xanax or, back in my drinking days, getting blackout drunk. The only time I ever felt safe flying was when I was in the Marine Corps on the way to the Middle East in support of Operation Iraqi Freedom. We had traveled in a chartered commercial plane with our weapons on board. Although completely irrational, I had felt safe knowing I had my M16 resting on the floor in between my feet. What help that would be if the plane went down (which was my real fear), I have no idea. Once again, these are the thoughts of the irrational, fearful mind.

As I said, for years I struggled with this terrifying fear of flying, to the point of missing out on incredible trips. I remember once when I was living in Germany, I booked a weekend trip to London to meet up with a girlfriend. A few days before the trip the nightmares were so bad, I canceled. To this day I'm still salty at myself for missing a chance to roll up in front of Buckingham Palace and say, "What's up?" to Her Majesty the Queen. Who knows? Maybe it would have been my picture in front of the palace that would have helped me manifest marrying Prince Harry. But Meghan Markle got on the plane and I didn't. So there's that.

Finally, after years of drug- and alcohol-induced comas on planes and missing out on amazing trips, I decided I needed to get rid of my fear of flying once and for all. I did what all the experts suggested: I learned everything I could about how planes work. I learned about the speed and force necessary to get a plane off the ground. I learned about the various, perfectly natural sounds an aircraft makes at different points in a journey. I learned that a plane can handle losing an engine and that it can even land safely, albeit bumpily, without any landing gear. When I tell you I learned everything I could, I mean *everything*. And that helped for a bit. Whenever I would get on a plane, I breathed deeply and simply reminded myself that the sounds were normal and that the average plane and its wings could withstand a significant amount of turbulence before anything catastrophic would happen. But I still didn't feel *peace*. I wanted to get to the point where I could get on an airplane and feel utter peace.

Peace comes when we surrender. Leading up to my next trip, I decided this was it, I was absolutely done with being so afraid of a situation I had very little control over. That's how I developed the All Outcomes Matrix. It's not nearly as fancy as it sounds, yet it's highly effective. It's a matter of asking the best questions for the circumstance. I had to remind myself that at the end of the day, the only thing I could control were my thoughts, and ultimately how I chose to view the situation. At the end of the day, surrender was an option for me only after I considered and accepted all possible out-comes. In the case of flying, I had to think about all of what could happen as a result of getting on a plane.

What's the best possible outcome of getting on a plane? Well, that's easy. The best-case scenario is that I land safely and life car-ries on. Who knows? Maybe that's the trip that lets me scratch off a dream destination from my bucket list. Am I okay with that? Yup! That would be fantastic. The best possible outcome is landing safely, and that would be great for me.

Okay, the next question I asked myself was, what's the worst possible outcome? Whoa, yikes. The worst possible outcome is the plane crashes and nobody survives. Am I okay with that? At first, I wasn't okay with that at all. That was my biggest fear, and I had to ask myself: *Why am I afraid of this? Why am I so scared of the worst-case outcome?* That day on the plane back from Florida, when the airplane dropped and I saw the wing of the plane and the ocean water getting too close for my comfort, the one and only thought that crossed my mind was *Oh my God, no! I can't leave my mom.* She was my biggest concern. Although she was a grown woman, I couldn't help but feel empathy for the devastation I knew she'd experience if anything were to happen to me.

Years later, after becoming a mom myself and still struggling with my fear of flying, I was no longer as concerned about my mom and instead my fear was leaving my babies behind. As I practiced the All Outcomes Matrix, once again I asked myself, *Am I okay with the worst-case scenario?* No. I was not. I remember thinking, *I want to see my children grow up. I want to be there for them. I don't want to leave my husband with that responsibility, all by himself. I am not okay with this possibility.*

Rather than force myself into feeling okay with it, I moved on to the next possibilities. What are the in-between possible outcomes? Some may argue that life is black-and-white, but I believe the world has a lot of gray, nuanced in-betweenness. In this example, one in-between possible outcome is that the plane crashes, we all survive, and then I'm even more traumatized than when I first got on the plane. Oddly enough, I was okay with that outcome. I rationalized that was because I'd still be alive and able to continue working on this phobia.

ALIGNMENT OPPORTUNITY

What's one thing you want to take action on but fear keeps holding you back? Choose an area in which your truth might invite judgment and potentially offend someone. Got it? Okay, good. Now let's put it up against the All Outcomes Matrix.

The action I fear taking is . . .

What's the best outcome?

What's the worst outcome?

What are the in-between possible outcomes?

Am I okay with these possible outcomes?

What is required for me to be okay?

If I'm not okay, am I willing to get to a place of surrendering to the things I cannot control?

I took it a step further and listed every other possibility and its outcome, including getting hijacked—God forbid! I kept going until I got to a point where I was okay with every outcome, except the worst-case scenario in which the plane crashes and no one survives. Having that one possibility lingering over my head, I asked myself, *What will it take for me to be okay with this possible outcome?*

To be honest, years later, I'm still not okay with it. My desire and intention is to live a very, very long, healthy life. My intention is to live into my nineties at least. Yet I understand that there are certain things I cannot control. My choices are in my control. I can choose to get on a plane or I can choose to forfeit some of my dreams of travel and adventure. I can choose to live an exceptional life or I can choose to settle for what I consider to be mediocrity because my fears and worries have gotten the best of me. Here's where I landed on the plane situation and why now I'm able to fly with ease and actually enjoy an experience that once terrified me. All of my affairs are in order. If, God forbid, something happens to me, I know my children will be taken care of. I know that I have salvation and that I'll be in heaven, kiki-ing it up with the angels and having a big ol' booming house party with my Creator. I'm in no rush to get there, and still, I trust God's sovereign plan. I understand that I won't be able to understand all things. I'm willing to accept the things that I cannot control. *That* is how you navigate the All Outcomes Matrix.

I chose to share this story of my past mega airplane phobia because I wanted you to see an extreme example of how helpful this tool can be. It's also helpful when it comes to scary and less gloomy, doomy outcomes, like posting on social media or asking your boss for a raise or taking a stand against an injustice you witnessed. Try it!

The All Outcomes Matrix is about accepting all the possibilities. It's the first step of faith required to embody the Empathetic Offender identity. Once you've accepted your truth, your next step to living in high faith is learning how to surrender. The difference between acceptance and surrender is that when you step into surrender, you allow yourself to *feel* the emotions. When you work through the All Outcomes Matrix, you use reasoning and rational cognitive processes to achieve acceptance. As you enter into surrender, you harmonize reasoning with emotions.

SURRENDER

When my first daughter was born, I was still on active duty in the US Marine Corps. I had worked my way up the ranks to E-6 (to give you an idea, the enlisted rank structure goes up to E-9—I was close!). On the morning of July 28, 2008, I walked into my office in Stuttgart, Germany, for my regular workday. My baby wasn't due until August 8th, and I had no intention of taking any time off prior to the baby's arrival. I wanted to prove to my bosses that I was a hard charger and that they could count on me to lead our Marines, even though I could no longer see my toes. Later that evening I went into labor, and the very next morning my daughter was born. Thirty-two days later, I was back in my office, ready for work. I would have rushed back sooner if not for the fact that no day care would take babies less than thirty days old. A friend was kind enough to keep my baby girl while I raced back to the office to prove myself and my worth to our team.

I loved my job, but before my baby turned a year old, I was faced with a major decision: stay in the Marine Corps and get reassigned back to the States or accept an honorable discharge and stay in Germany with my husband. Important to note: at the time, we were not yet married, so the Marine Corps wasn't obligated to transfer me near him. I chose my family.

By the time Isabella was headed to kindergarten, I had been in business just under three years. Things were going well, so I decided to join the PTA, sign up as a class co-mom, and attempt to live out the fairy-tale family dream I had seen growing up on television. I don't know what the heck I was thinking! For starters, I don't like cleaning up after people, and every time I'd set out to do baking or crafts with the kids, the mess would drive me crazy. Secondly, I'm not really into kids like that. I love *my* kids and babies six months and under. Once babies are mobile and can talk back, I'm out. I had *no* business being a class co-mom or volunteering to help *inside* the classroom. It was stress after stress after stress. Not to mention the fact that all this time with the kids was taking me away from my business—the one thing that was *mine*.

Running my business and working with my clients gave me a sense of joy and fulfillment that I didn't find in motherhood. If anything, I found motherhood (at that time) to be a bait-and-switch experience. I had been sold a dream. "When you see your child for the first time, you'll feel love you never thought was possible," I had been told. That's not what I felt! When Isabella was born, all I felt was fear. I wasn't ready to be a mom. I wasn't ready for the responsibility. And when the doctors found what they suspected to be a tumor and she was taken to the neonatal ICU just days after she was born, that fear only intensified. No, I didn't feel overwhelming love at the birth of my daughter. I felt fear and responsibility. Thankfully the so-called tumor turned out to be just a swollen gland from the difficult delivery. The doctors assured me she'd be fine (and she was), but I was still wounded from the experience.

Twenty-three months later, when my second daughter was born, I thought I'd have a do-over. Maybe *this* time I'd get to feel that euphoric love I'd been told about. Nope. This time I felt relief. The labor and delivery had been so easy, only forty-five minutes from start to finish, compared to twelve hours with my first. Still, no overwhelming feeling of endless love. Just relief it had been easy, and *guilt* for not feeling that love. This was such a painful experience. Two times I had been betrayed by the idea of motherhood. Where were the books and movies and stories about *this* kind of motherhood? Nowhere to be found in my world, that's for sure.

As the girls grew older, I really tried to be the "perfect" mom *and* businesswoman in hopes that one day everything I had been told about being a mom would be true for me. It wasn't until several years later—after invariably defending myself to other moms who didn't understand why I wanted my career *and* to have a family—that it hit me: I had to surrender and accept that I was never going to be the mother I'd thought I'd be or that others wanted me to be.

Growing up, I had thought I was going to be the kind of mom who baked cookies and cakes with her children. The kind of mom who did arts and crafts, signed up for the PTA, and was a class co-mom. And I tried. I really did. But I have never valued doing things for the sole purpose of looking good in the eyes of others. I value doing things for fulfillment, not out of obligation. As soon as I made the decision to surrender what I thought motherhood should be and leaned into what I wanted my relationship with my children to be, *everything shifted.*

In my state of surrender, I simply thought, *This is me. I'm not the kind of mom I thought I'd be, and I'm okay with that. I'm no longer judging myself. I don't care what anyone else says. I'm no longer judging my feelings. Whether my fears and insecurities around motherhood stay or go, I am safe.*

That's how I discovered that our connection to living in a truly supportive community is birthed when we surrender and speak authentically. I began to speak my honest truth about motherhood and the unintentional feelings of resentment I felt toward my children. I spoke about the guilt I felt for wanting my own identity outside my role as a mom. I began asking other moms who were better at mothering for support. Suddenly I was surrounded by moms who felt the same way as I did—yay, community!—as well as moms who were amazing at showing me how I could be loving, nurturing, *and* true to myself. Not only that, but now that I had my truth and a community of moms who respected and accepted that truth, my relationship with my daughters completely changed. I *finally* got to feel that all-consuming love for my daughters. But it was made possible only when I surrendered. My dreams, desires, beliefs, and values would not always be "right" for others, so I surrendered the desire to "get it right" and embraced getting aligned with my truth. You can too:

Surrender your wounds.

Surrender the need to be validated.

Surrender wanting to control the narrative others create.

Surrender the desire to be accepted by people who don't share your beliefs or values.

Simply, surrender.

─────── **AFFIRMATION** ───────────

IT'S SAFE FOR ME TO RISK MY REPUTATION AND SURRENDER THE NEED TO BE VALIDATED BY OTHERS.

──────────────────── #PermissiontoOffend ─────────

PRINCIPLES OF RISKING YOUR REPUTATION

▶ You must be willing to risk your reputation in order to step into the next iteration of who you really are.

▶ In order to risk, you must release your emotional attachment to the outcomes.

▶ Routinely using the All Outcomes Matrix is key to releasing your attachments.

▶ Peace comes only when you surrender. Surrender and accept all of who you are now so you can embrace who you are becoming.

Surrender requires faith and acceptance. Can you fully accept your own personal truth, and will you surrender any and all ideas that no longer align with that truth? If you can, you'll be able to enjoy the freedom I know you're ready to experience. Let's go there now.

PART 3

I GIVE MYSELF PERMISSION TO LIVE IN FREEDOM

For you were called to freedom, brothers. Only do not use your freedom as an opportunity for the flesh, but through love serve one another.

—GALATIANS 5:13, ESV

8

OFFEND WITH INTENTION

"I love ya, Rach, but ya gotta stop talking about God so much!" my dear friend Jess said to me one day, many years ago, when I was first starting my business. I was like the young aspiring actress from a small town in Middle America who, with stars in her eyes, moves out to Hollywood thinking she's going to be discovered as soon as she steps off the bus. I believed starting a business would be easy and that as long as I was true to myself, gave value, and helped others, I'd build my empire in no time.

"What do you mean, stop talking about God so much?" I asked.

"People don't wanna hear about that. They don't want to be preached at. You're going to offend and alienate people," Jess said.

"What are you talking about? I'm not preachy. When have I ever been preachy?"

Between you and me, at the time I was quite offended. Back then I didn't know anything about increasing my Offense Capacity Quotient, and I felt some type of way about the idea that I might be coming across as "preachy."

"Well, you're not. But still. No one wants to hear about God when they are looking to hire a coach," she said matter-of-factly.

I pushed back a little by saying, "But I don't talk about God in my sessions unless a client is a Christian and *she* brings it up. I know how to separate church and state. And anyway, don't I *want* to alienate anyone who isn't a good fit for me?"

Jess and I had met in an online marketing program, and one of the major messages we were learning was the importance of "niching down," or finding the people in a marketplace who share your beliefs and values. Wasn't talking about my beliefs a sign that I was implementing what we were being taught? I was confused, to say the least.

Because Jess seemed to have more online business experience than I did, I listened to her. That turned out to be a pretty big mistake. It's not that her advice wasn't sound. It's that it took me so far from my identity that I constantly battled with imposter syndrome and struggled to get clear on my message. I felt like I was hiding this really big part of myself to make others feel comfortable. In the process, I was extremely uncomfortable in my own business. Not to mention my revenue dropped dramatically. Eventually I decided I needed to lean into my personal truth and give myself *permission to offend*. Guess what happened next. My revenue grew exponentially. How's that for proof?

Now when someone tells me to stop talking about God so much because I might alienate or offend people, I thank them for sharing their opinion and keep it moving. Because to not offend a human, by default, causes me to offend my God. My salvation is not up for negotiation, no matter how offensive that may seem to some. To reiterate: I'm not emotionally attached to who you choose to serve or not serve. Nor am I interested in converting you. I'm interested in living fully expressed and learning more about you so we can find points of connection that will bring us together for the greater good of humanity.

Shying away and not being willing to offend in defense of your truth can be detrimental to your identity, mission, and purpose.

Think about the last time you wanted to do something really important to you but you didn't speak up or stand your ground because you were worried about offending someone (or being judged, rejected, and/or defamed). How did you feel? Were you in flow? Were you in alignment? Did you feel like you were living in full freedom? Probably not. This chapter is going to help you with that. It *is* possible to speak your truth and still enjoy healthy relationships with people who share different beliefs and values.

I don't know if I'd say there's an appropriate moment to offend someone, but I know for darn skippy there is such a thing as a *necessary* moment. We live with a false sense of security and certainty that we have plenty of time. We often procrastinate having difficult conversations and make excuses like "I don't want to hurt them," "I'll wait for a time when they're in a better mood," "It's better for me to just keep this to myself," thinking we will have a chance later. None of us are promised tomorrow and yet we procrastinate as if we've got some sort of guarantee.

Saving others from pain will cost you your own growth and will, by default, keep you in a comfort zone. Ask yourself, *What's more important, my comfort or my truth?*

OFFENDING THE PEOPLE YOU LOVE

"My parents are my biggest fans," Katie said. "We have a great relationship, and they consume my content on social media. It's great! The problem is that by stepping up and sharing my truth, it's caused my parents to be triggered by some of my content. I've grown immensely because of how I've been showing up, but how do I tell these stories without blasting them?"

She continued: "I've gotten to a point where I recognize that people come into our world and do us 'harm' but the harm actually helps our growth. I want to honor them by sharing authentically without throwing them under the bus."

Katie's concern isn't an unusual one. In truth, one of the most frequently asked questions I get is "How do I do and say what I want without hurting or losing people?"

Like Katie, this was a major concern for Amanda. She had already rocked the family boat by choosing to leave the Mormon faith. Now she wanted to share more of her story online but worried about the impact her personal truth would have on her family, especially her mom who was already quite offended by Amanda's use of swear words. But this—her sharing about the temple, something that was so sacred and dear to her mother's identity—was taking things to another level.

I don't know anything about being Mormon, but from what Amanda told me, there are many beautiful traditions that are to be kept private. Telling her story would mean potentially exposing these cherished secrets which would hurt her mom in one of the worst possible ways.

Nevertheless, vowing to stand up for her truth, Amanda shared a post on social media announcing that she and her husband were renewing their vows after ten years of marriage. Although she had married her best friend, Amanda wrote in her post, "Everything about that day is filled with trauma and grief to me. I lost my youth. My identity. My dreams. It probably doesn't make sense to anyone who wasn't raised Mormon—or anyone who still identifies as Mormon—but I was given a new name, vowed to have children, to listen and to obey my husband, to wear special underwear, among other things. Even sharing that feels dirty because I was sworn to secrecy." She added a small parenthetical to her post: "(this is my story and I have a right to share it)." That last sentence was Amanda doing her best to validate as well as defend herself.

Seeing this post, and knowing what a big deal this was, I called her right away and said, "I'm proud of you, friend." Actually, what I first said was "I'm not crying, you're crying!" Then we laughed and *then* I told her I was proud of her. Over the two years since I had first coached her and our friendship began to forge, I had seen Amanda step out of her comfort zone one small step at a time. Little by little Amanda had shared more and more of her true identity. She worked diligently to get clear on what she believed and what she valued. The more clarity she gained on what she *actually* believed, as opposed to what she was taught to believe, the more bold faith she had.

Posting about her marriage was a daring move for Amanda, especially since her mother had already called her earlier in the day about another post that contained a curse word to tell her, "that was offensive." It's no wonder Amanda had been nervous to share about her vow renewal. The comment her mother had made earlier in the day was still fresh in her mind, so I reminded her, "Your truth is not offensive. She is offended. There's a difference . . . Remember, when you speak your truth, it causes others to question their own values and beliefs. Their identity is in question, and that can be scary. Grace and empathy for both of you."

Our conversation continued, and when I asked her who all was invited to the vow renewal, practically demanding my invitation, she said, "It's just going to be us and the kids, which makes me sad because I thought about who I would really want there. I'd want my sisters and my mom. But they are still in the faith and they don't understand. It would almost be pointless, and I don't want to invite my closest friends and not my family . . ." Her voice trailed off.

"I just want to be told, 'I'm proud of you,'" she added.

Feeling her pain, I said, "Friend, please don't mistake their lack of understanding as being a lack of pride for you and what you've achieved. Why are you making it mean that? Isn't it possible that your family is incredibly proud of you and maybe they even admire how bold and courageous you are? Remember, your truth challenges their truth. Asking them to celebrate your truth, a truth that goes against their fundamental beliefs, is asking them to betray their identity. You've worked for years to find your identity. Would you want them to ask you to celebrate the parts of the faith that you are now fundamentally opposed to?"

"No. You're right," Amanda said with calm resolution. "I'm really proud of myself for speaking up, and I've gotten so much support from so many women both in and outside the Mormon faith. Other women really needed this."

That is the gift of the *Permission to Offend* movement. It goes beyond us. It's how we give voices to the voiceless. It's how we learn to bridge the gaps between differences of beliefs, values, cultures, and economic systems. It's how we grow together. Make no mistake: this never has been and never will be about blatantly disrespecting others. Giving yourself *permission to offend* will always be about standing up to honor your values and beliefs—with empathy, compassion, understanding, and mutual respect.

Incidentally, the more she gave herself *permission to offend*, the more Amanda's business grew. During the time we worked together,

ALIGNMENT OPPORTUNITY

Practice saying the following statements out loud. Let them serve as a reminder when navigating difficult conversations that trigger offense.

"Your truth doesn't make me a liar. My truth doesn't make you a liar. We simply hold different beliefs. If we want to coexist and cocreate, all we need to do is find a thread to unify us despite our differences."

There will most certainly be moments in life when you'll be called to work with someone whose beliefs, values, opinions, or ideologies absolutely contradict your own. Remember these statements, stand in your truth, and keep it moving.

Amanda scaled her business revenue from $250,000 per year to over $1 million. It's amazing how your entire life changes when you operate in high personal truth and high faith.

Every situation is different, so while there isn't one standard way to "offend" with minimal collateral damage, I'm going to do my best to give you some strategies to handle various situations. There are nine core principles to consider when you're walking in your truth.

1. COMMUNICATE YOUR INTENT.

Offending people can easily be avoided by communicating your intent. The opportunity for offending someone is greatest when you don't take the time to engage in a real conversation about what's important to you and how the things that matter to you might affect them.

Have you ever heard someone say, "That wasn't my intention," then heard them be told, "It's not about intent. It's about impact"? Having an up-front conversation can help generate a much better outcome.

2. ENROLL OTHERS IN YOUR VISION.

Once you've shared your intent, the next step is to enroll others in your vision. This means showing what's possible as a result of you saying, doing, and/or being whatever you want. During this step, you might also consider sharing why whatever you want to say, do, and/or be is important to you and how it benefits others (if at all).

This step is really more for conversations with family, partners, friends, and loved ones. But in full transparency, I personally have, on a few occasions, communicated my intent and vision with my clients and students before I've shared things on social media.

This step matters because it helps contribute to ensuring the impact matches your intent. I've seen so many situations that easily could have been avoided by a person communicating their intent and enrolling others in their vision *before* setting out to speak their piece.

These first two steps truly do require you to have faith and willingness to shake things up. Look, at some point or another you're going to be uncomfortable. Rip the Band-Aid off, get uncomfortable, walk across the fire.

3. ASSESS THE SITUATION.

Remember the All Outcomes Matrix? This principle is a nod to that. Now that you've communicated intent and (hopefully) enrolled others in your vision, you get to assess their responses. If your intent was well received, then fantastic. Keep moving forward with your plans and take that freedom walk in the direction of your desires. If, however, you were met with opposition, then it's time to assess the situation.

- How did the conversation go? Remember to separate the facts from your stories.
- Were you open and honest throughout the entire conversation or did you find yourself holding back? What was left unsaid? What could you have done differently?
- How did the conversation end? Is there an alternate ending you would have preferred? Were any agreements made?

Take mental notes but also grab a notebook and write down what happened. Document the difficult. Pay attention to how your body is feeling. Remember, the body is capable of experiencing emotions before the mind is consciously aware of thoughts replaying in the subconscious. Here are a few things you can do to check in:

- Slow down and take a breath.
- Starting at the top of your head, check and see if your eyebrows are furrowed or if your jaw is locked.
- Check in with your throat. Does it feel tight or is it relaxed? Do you feel any tension in your neck?
- Move down to your shoulders and notice if they're shrugged. How's your chest feeling? Any tightness or pressure?
- What about your back? Any muscle pain coming through?
- Continue scanning down your body, and pay attention to your heartbeat. Is it fast, slow, or steady?
- How's your tummy? Does it feel queasy or flip-floppy? Do you have butterflies?

Make your way through your body and simply notice what's coming up for you. You're looking to see where you feel anything out of the ordinary so that you can separate the truth from the story around those feelings. Take notes. Keep practicing. After a while this will become automatic, and the more you work through the emotions in your body, the quicker you will be able to release the unnecessary feelings holding you back.

To access an audio file on which I guide you through a body scan, visit www.permissiontooffend.com/more.

4. CHECK IN WITH YOUR IDENTITY.

You remember this from earlier, but let's review. What do you believe? Have you stayed true to your beliefs? What do you value?

Have you stayed true to those values? Can you look in the mirror and think good thoughts about your beliefs and values? Making this a daily practice is a step toward living in freedom.

5. MAKE A DECISION AND MAKE IT WORK.

One of the best bits of advice I've ever received is "Make a decision and make it work." A core belief I hold is that being double-minded makes you unstable. It causes you to constantly question yourself and doubt your abilities, and it keeps you stuck when you should be moving forward. This belief, coupled with an affirmation to make decisions and make them work, helps keep me accountable to my actions. Try it for yourself and watch things shift.

6. TAKE RESPONSIBILITY FOR YOUR IMPACT.

In a moment we'll talk more in-depth about damage control when your offense causes harm, but the core of that is taking full responsibility and accountability for your impact. You can minimize negative impact by being clear in your intention and considering the All Outcomes Matrix we covered in chapter 7. Apologize when warranted and simply own it.

7. RESIST THE URGE TO DEFEND YOUR INTENTION.

Your intention is not on trial; the hurt that was caused is what's being examined and cross-examined. It's not always easy, but try your best not to convince the other person to understand your intention. When someone is hurt, they don't care about your intention; they care about how your words and actions made them feel. Give the person space to fully express themselves. Instead of rushing to defend your intention, try some of these statements:

I'm sorry you were hurt by my actions or words.

I understand what I did or said hurt you and I'm sorry.

Thank you for sharing your feelings with me.

These are statements of empathy, which you can find more examples of in chapter 10.

8. RELEASE YOUR EMOTIONAL ATTACHMENT TO THE OUTCOME.

You know how to do this. Before you do the scary thing that might cause offense, go through the All Outcomes Matrix from chapter 7 and surrender. Go back to your identity. Who do you want to be? How do you want to show up in the world? Live in your truth and walk in faith. To quote the Disney princess Elsa, "Let it go!"

9. OFFEND IN DEFENSE OF YOUR TRUTH.

Remember, these nine principles aren't about asking anyone for permission to be, do, or say the things you want. These are strategies, if you will, to help you achieve your intended outcome and impact. Make no mistake: there will be moments when you do your absolute best to honor others and they are still not satisfied. That's when you need to make a decision and make it work. Will you risk offending in defense of your truth?

There *will* be times when you choose not to offend. There *will* be moments when you choose to avoid hurting someone, not because you're afraid they'll reject you—you know they won't—but because you simply don't want them to hurt. When that day comes, it will mean only what you make it mean.

There were a few stories I really wanted to share with you in this book but I didn't because telling them would have a greater negative impact on people I care about than the impact of inspiring you. Consider your impact. Recall the All Outcomes Matrix and think about all the possibilities. Which possibility aligns most with your identity? Now that you're reading this book and doing the work, trust that you'll know exactly when it's time for you to offend and when it's more authentic for you to choose another path. It's safe for you to believe that when you stand in your truth it's not gratuitous.

Remember Amanda? She wanted and needed to hear someone tell her, "I'm so proud of you for standing in your truth." I hope I can be that person for you.

Real talk: Whenever I read books where the author gives a pep talk, I kind of cringe. I think, *I don't need your rah-rah, fluffy BS; I need you to tell me how to do the thing and show me what's necessary for my transformation.* Hopefully I've given you plenty of action steps that warrant this pep talk, because it's important you know someone in this world is celebrating you for honoring your truth.

I am proud of you. For real, for real. I celebrate you! Taking the time to learn and implement the tools in this book isn't easy. Actually going out into the world, living your truth, and giving yourself permission to offend is *scary* and it takes massive amounts of courage. But the world, now more than ever, *needs you and your voice!* We need you speaking up and out against injustice. We need you setting the example for our younger generation to help them feel more at ease with their true identity. We need *you* to be the voice of change in

boardrooms that oppress and suppress disenfranchised and marginalized communities. On the reals, *we need you to offend in support of
your truth.* Thank you for being willing to step into the fire and blaze
the trail.

MORE THAN WORDS

"It's not just what she said, it's *how* she said it."

A popular influencer on social media had come under fire for
things she had said on camera about her lifestyle. As I watched the
footage, I understood why so many people were outraged and what
they'd meant when they said, "It's not just what she said, it's *how* she
said it." When it comes to speaking up and out, standing in your
truth, and using your voice for change, it's important to consider not
only the words you use but also the *way* you say them. Your emotions
and energy can affect your tone. If you're a very passionate person,
your tone might come across as mad or angry when in reality you're
just excited or engaged. Some things to consider when speaking your
truth are body language, facial expression, and tonality. These all
help your audience create meaning from the words you're using. As
you start taking the bold steps to speak your truth, *practice!!!* Look at
yourself in the mirror or, better yet, record yourself on video as you
speak your truth. Does your tone reflect your intention? If you're
using a written modality like email or text messages to express yourself, send it to a trusted friend first and give them some verification
metrics. You can ask things like:

What tone did you hear when you read this?

How did you feel as you read it? Were you surprised, angry, annoyed?

Does any of this bring up any negative or positive feelings?

Come up with your own metrics for verification and give it a try. When it comes to body, face, and tone, use the following table as a quick reference guide.

	BODY LANGUAGE	FACIAL EXPRESSIONS	TONALITY
POSITIVE	Arms uncrossed	Eye contact gentle	Kindness
	Open hands	Mouth smiling	Lightness
	Head nodding	Head tilting	Warmth
			Understanding
NEGATIVE	Finger pointing	Eyes glaring	Sarcasm
	Frowning	Nose wrinkling	Condescension
	Eyes rolling	Eyebrows furrowed	Smugness
	Hands fisted or clasped	Lips tight or a corner of the mouth raised	Dismissiveness

Finally, another thing to consider: Is what you're saying aligned with what you've said and how you've shown up in the past? In my opinion, one of the other main reasons the audience was so upset with the social media influencer was because she was saying things contrary to the identity she had portrayed in past years. There was no enrollment for the audience, letting them know changes were coming. Therefore, this new message felt out of alignment. Suddenly what they had perceived to be true all these years was called into question. The audience's collective foundation was shaken.

Just like the entire identity of Amanda's mom was called into question when Amanda began speaking her truth, when you start showing up outside the character and identity others have become accustomed to, some won't be able to handle it. This is where enrolling others in your vision is helpful. Obviously it's perfectly acceptable to pivot and start walking in a new truth. Just remember to communicate and enroll others in the ideas you have so they know what to expect from you moving forward. Explanations are an offering, not a debt. You don't *owe* anyone any explanations or justifications, but giving a heads-up certainly does help minimize negative impact.

DAMAGE CONTROL

(Trigger warning: a brief mention of abuse coming up.)

Let's say, just for fun and giggles, that as you're walking in your truth, something goes all the way wrong. You did it. You were brave. You had your big-girl panties on and said what you said. Uh-oh! Something you said has truly been harmful and problematic to a marginalized community. Or maybe you spoke up and finally told the truth about the person who sexually abused you. Now the whole family is mad at you for exposing the secret. Major damage has been done. Not only have you offended people but also your testimony has caused great harm and led to fractured relationships. Now you find yourself questioning all your life decisions, wondering, *Should I have even given myself permission to offend?*

The answer (in my humble opinion) is, *Yes!!!* Although I think there will always be some people who don't believe there is ever a time to give yourself permission to offend, I believe the world desperately needs more people who are willing to stand up and speak out. The world needs more of *your authentic truth*. Let's also remember that speaking up leads to freedom, not just for yourself but for others as well. Please keep that in mind. Let's universally agree that no matter how perfectly you follow the principles outlined in this book, there's a chance someone will be not only offended but also hurt by the activation and expression of your truth.

Personally, I believe offense is a choice. Let me explain: We've already discussed how automated our thoughts can be. So it's fair to say that something will be said that triggers an automatic thought of offense. But it's a *choice* to stay in the energy and emotion of offense. We all get to choose how we want to navigate through life's circumstances, which is why we began in chapter 1 with separating our thoughts, feelings, stories, and facts around each situation.

Permission Slip

I give myself permission to activate my truth.

#PermissiontoOffend

Now that we've gotten that out of the way, let's figure this out. All hell has broken loose. Now what? If you find yourself needing to do damage control, start with taking a moment to pause and breathe. Resist the temptation to react, and instead take a moment to carefully check in with yourself, your truth, your identity, your values, your beliefs. Ask yourself, *Does this relationship matter enough to me to warrant a response?* Not every relationship is worth the effort required to do damage control. There. I said it. You get to decide which ones are worth investing the time, effort, and emotional energy into repairing. Sometimes we hold on to relationships past their expiration date, hoping things will change. How people respond to your truth is a reflection of whether or not it's time to let it go. Likewise, you'll have to accept that people will choose to let go of *you.*

If the answer is, *Yes, this relationship matters to me, and I want to preserve it,* then the first step is to acknowledge the hurt, without being defensive, making excuses, or attempting to justify your actions. I get it. We all want to be right. We want to defend our truth, and this whole time I have taught you that every step of the way you are giving yourself permission to offend in defense of your truth. And also, there are times when you need to take a moment to listen and acknowledge. People want to be seen and heard. By acknowledging that you've caused pain, without justifying or defending yourself, you are extending the first olive branch that may lead to reparation in the relationship.

The second step is to set parameters around which you're willing to engage in a healthy dialogue. For example, if you're feeling scared, sensitive, emotional, or any other feeling around the fact that your truth has caused damage, ask for time and grace. Often conflicts are not resolved efficiently or effectively because the party who has been hurtful does not acknowledge the hurt or ask for the time they need to gather themselves or evaluate their actions. Here are some phrases to add to your handbag for when you're on the go and things hit the fan:

I am sorry. Please give me grace. I would like some time to think and be thoughtful in my response.

I want to give you a loving, thoughtful response. I don't want to react defensively or minimize your feelings.

Are you willing to give me some time to really think about what I've done and/or said so that we can come to an understanding?

I would like X amount of time to think and process. Let's have lunch [give a specific date and time], if you're available. I really appreciate your support in this.

Taking a moment to explain why you want and need time to reflect helps the other person start to have a better understanding of the situation. Some people, like myself, are verbal processors. Intrinsically, I want to talk things out right then and there because it's quite noisy in my mind. Other people are introspective processors. They need to go to a quiet place and privately process before they can open up. Know yourself and your audience. If they are verbal processors, acknowledge that. Try saying something like "I know you prefer to process things right in the moment and talk through every little detail. I'm willing to do that with you after I've had some time to get my thoughts together."

Affirming the other person is a great way to do damage control. By doing so, you get ahead of whatever story they might start telling themselves. Offer up something like "I want to make sure you understand why I'm not ready to talk just yet. It has nothing to do with you. This is who I am and how I process. I need some time to myself. It doesn't mean [*insert whatever potential story they might have*]. I care about you, and because I care, I want to be thoughtful, intentional, and respectful when we speak."

Trust me when I say, I *know* how much patience and practice this requires. By nature, I'm a real hothead, so doing this work and teaching it to you now has been quite the journey. Sometimes, in the heat of the moment, you may want to defer to your first response, but I assure you, that's almost *never* the best route. One of the reasons why I encourage you to read this book more than once is because you need to get into repetition. Repetition is the key to mastery. If you're reacting in the heat of the moment, having mastered these key phrases can help with damage control.

Communicating and expressing your needs goes a long way when it comes to living the *Permission to Offend* lifestyle. You might be surprised to learn how understanding people are willing to be when you communicate. It's when you ghost someone or stay quiet that people have real problems. I'm going to say it again: people want to be seen and heard. They want to believe that you understand what you did or said was hurtful to them. Even if it is your truth, there may very well be a case in which someone feels hurt and/or offended. In fact, let me take this moment right now to acknowledge that there may have been things in this book that have offended and/or hurt you. If that is the case, I am genuinely sorry my work caused harm. I apologize. My truth doesn't make your truth a lie. I believe that and hope you do as well.

Shall we go on? There's another phrase I'd love for you to add to your memory bank: "I'm available for dialogue. Let's discuss."

Practice saying this with me right now: "I'm available for dialogue. Let's discuss."

This phrase is so helpful to use when someone is really mad and they have automatically assumed in their mind that you couldn't possibly see their point of view. When you hit them with an "I'm available for dialogue. Let's discuss," ooooh-weee, you stun them. This is one of those responses you'll want to quickly grab from your mental back pocket when you're in the middle of a heated conversation. Another good one is "Let's communicate and see how we can work this out." Try either of these the next time you're doing damage control.

All right, moving on. You've acknowledged and apologized for their pain without compromising your values or your beliefs. You've set clear parameters by asking for what you need and offered a thoughtful response. Now it's time to consider the feedback the other person is giving you:

Are they upset with what I said or with how I said it?

Are they upset because I have a fundamentally different belief or perspective?

Is there an underlying fear or irrational thought coming up for them?

What did the person actually say when they called you offensive or whatever words they threw your way? Resist the urge to infer what they meant. Consider only what they said. If you are not sure what they meant, go back and ask. Do not make the mistake of allowing your story to get in the way of hearing their truth. Pause. Ask for clarification. Here's an example: "You've mentioned I didn't celebrate your achievements and that hurt you. What can I do the next time to help you feel more loved, honored, and celebrated?" Most people don't think to ask the person, "This is what you said, this is what I think you meant. Am I correct?" Asking that question alone will give the other person an indication that you are trying to understand where they're coming from.

Finally, examine their concerns against your beliefs, values, and identity as a whole. Is there an opportunity for you to acknowledge, take responsibility, apologize, and lay out the steps for how you will do better? Or is this a moment when you are going to double down on what is true and authentic for you? Is this one of those times when you tell yourself, *Whatever. They're hurt and choosing to stay hurt. I've apologized. I'm moving on.* The latter is a little harder to do. It takes a lot of consideration, and it can be nuanced depending on who the person is and how deeply interconnected your relationship is. This is also the option you might want to employ if someone has ghosted you despite your attempts to engage in meaningful conversation. Being ghosted is painful, but if you've done your part to reconcile and they aren't responding—at some point you have to let people be who they are.

Here are some other introspective questions you can journal around:

What is the most productive way I can respond that aligns with my identity?

Did I operate from my stories or from the facts? Which stories do I need to own up to?

Where is my responsibility in their pain? (Note that you may not bear any responsibility for their pain, but it's still a good question to ask yourself.)

What can I say or do that allows me to stay in my truth while also acknowledging the hurt that has been caused?

Whether you're taking on new beliefs or vocalizing your true, often hidden beliefs, you might find people who deeply care about you will be resistant to your change because your truth no longer aligns with theirs. When you change or say something that is contrary to everything you've ever done or said before, it causes the other person to question themselves and wonder, *Have I been wrong all along? Is it me?*

In some cases it might bring up thoughts for them like these: *You're not who I thought you were. Why are we in each other's lives? You've been deceiving me this entire time.*

In the case of Amanda's experience with her mom, by openly sharing her truth, it triggered her mom to think, *This is not how I raised you.* As a mom, I can personally relate to what I perceive to be an incredibly difficult situation for both women. I want my daughters to grow up to be strong, independent thinkers. Heck, they're the primary reasons I've written this book. I hope it teaches them how to speak up and out for causes that matter to them. At the same time, I'm raising them to believe in *my* God. I have a vision of them using prayer as a weapon to help them through life's challenges, just the way I've done. I have an expectation that they'll follow the scriptures I follow and believe as I believe, that the greatest commandment of all is to *love.* Should they grow up to choose a different belief system . . . well, quite frankly, it would be painful for me. I know my first thought which I would *never* verbalize because I get it—but I would *think* it!—would be, *You are not meeting the vision and expectation I had for how my life was going to look with you in it.* Personally, I am going to love my children through *everything*, but I would still feel the pain and grief of losing that vision.

As I shared my own perspective as a mother with Amanda, she

said, "Yes! My mom isn't afraid that she's going to lose me as a daughter. She's afraid she's gonna look at me and think, *I don't even know you. I didn't raise you to be this way.*"

When you give yourself permission to offend, it might trigger the death of a dream someone else had for your life. When you speak your truth, if they haven't worked on increasing their Offense Capacity Quotient, it can feel like a threat to their truth. When you actually start to follow your dreams, it may threaten their dreams. And who wants to be robbed of their dreams? No one! That's why you're doing this work. Because you're tired of not saying yes to your dreams. You're tired of living on other people's terms and conditions. You want to start calling your own shots. Right? If that's the case, then at some point you're going to have to draw a line in the sand and decide whose life you want to live. Are you going to live out *your* dreams or the dreams someone else has for you?

Personally, I don't believe life has to be this *or* that; it can be this *and* that. But in some cases you *really* do have to make a this-*or*-that decision. Choosing yourself doesn't mean you love or care less about the other person. What if it simply means you love yourself? Not more, not less—just that you love yourself and you're choosing yourself because this is *your* life.

And what if, as you begin to choose yourself and learn to have confident conversations—which are open dialogues about the common ground you share with someone—you usher in a new possibility? What if the new possibility is the opportunity to create a new dream together? That would be pretty awesome, wouldn't it?

Before we move forward, let me go on record to say: I 100 percent advocate standing in our truth, and also I advocate for opening our minds to the possibility of new beliefs and new values from time to time. Certain situations might require us to *at least consider* the possibility that our beliefs might be outdated. I mean, let's be real:

if people didn't question their beliefs during the suffrage and civil rights movements, our social landscape would be quite different. We *still* do not live in an "equal" society by any stretch of the imagination. But the progress we have today is a reflection of others having the courage to question and challenge their own beliefs. Please remember this the next time you see someone getting "called out" for being a gaslighter, racist, privileged, or any other noun or adjective that modifies a negative behavior you can't possibly see or imagine exhibited. Maybe it's true . . .

If it just so happens that you find yourself in a pickle, being called "problematic," or maybe you're aligned with someone who has been given said label, here are some questions to consider:

Are the beliefs I hold outdated?

What would I believe if I were in their exact situation?

If I hold true to my current beliefs, does it hinder or infringe upon someone else's human rights?

After you've taken the time to consider those questions, if your current beliefs still align with your values, well then . . . double down and keep moving forward. If they don't, then consider taking on new beliefs and follow the nine principles moving forward.

HOW TO APOLOGIZE

Does your situation warrant an apology? This is how you do it. Are you ready? Get your highlighter and then also write it down in your journal because writing helps us remember. This is what you say:

> "I'm sorry. I can see that I hurt you. I apologize."

That's it. Keep it brief. Don't take ownership over things that don't belong to you. The more you talk, the greater the chance you'll say something else that may cause further offense and harm.

If you must, and you absolutely cannot help yourself and feel like you need to add some extras, here's an option:

> "I'm sorry. I know that when I [insert a description of what you said or did], I hurt you. I apologize for the pain you're experiencing because of my words or actions. Going forward, I [insert what you will commit to doing to not cause the pain again]."

Seriously. That's it. Full stop right there.

INTENTION VS. IMPACT

My identity is rooted in love, and it is at the core of everything I desire to do, create, and experience. This is why I enjoy the confidence of knowing it's okay for me to be offensive. At the end of the day, my intentions are pure and the people who know me will know that. The person who doesn't know me but who is willing to do the work to create genuine connection and collaboration will take the time to *ask* about my intentions.

But it would be incredibly irresponsible of me not to address the difference between intention and impact. Sometimes our words and actions create an impact that doesn't align with our intention. In these situations it's important to take responsibility without owning blame, shame, or guilt. Following the nine principles outlined earlier in this chapter is helpful. More than anything, offering a *genuine apology* is critical. The best way you can ensure your impact aligns with your intention is to be thoughtful and informed. The more you know, hopefully the better you do.

THE NEW POSSIBILITY

"This *Permission to Offend* life is scary out here in these real streets," Athena said during one of our group calls. I love Athena! She's such a powerhouse, and she barely realizes it. Lately Athena has been stretching herself and "offending" left and right. She's raised her prices for her luxury handmade stationery company. She had the audacity to book herself a weekend getaway for her birthday without her husband or children *and* she even went so far as to not coordinate childcare or meals! She left it all up to her husband. *The nerve!* How offensive, right? *Not!!*

I hope you were able to hear my sarcasm as I shared all the incredible ways Athena is stepping into the Empathetic Offender identity while remaining true to her values and beliefs. Every week that passes, Athena blossoms and shifts right before my eyes. I'm so here for it—not just for Athena but for *you too!* And like she said, "This *Permission to Offend* life is scary." Let me encourage you. Yes, it *is* scary. It's also exhilarating and fun and makes you feel *alive!* The more you start walking in this life, the closer you'll get to the people, opportunities, and experiences that align with what you've always wanted and even some things you didn't know existed.

Remember earlier I mentioned the possibility of creating a new dream together? This has been the case with my husband and me. When we started dating, I don't remember us ever talking about our fundamental beliefs. We were too busy living it up in Europe, traveling, and living our best lives. I got pregnant. We had our first daughter and got married, and then life began happening. About three years into "real" married life and shortly after the birth of our second daughter, I realized, *Uh-oh. We don't actually believe the same things. Who is this guy?* To be fair to him, I know he's had similar thoughts about me over the years. As I grew more confident in my core beliefs and values and started speaking up even more than when he first met me—our foundation of what had brought us together was on really shaky ground. Neither of us recognized the other person.

This was scary—*for both of us.* Here I was, building my empire, running my mouth, and telling the world all my business on social media. Well, maybe not *all* my business, but enough to make him uncomfortable. At first I thought, *He's trying to silence me. He wants to keep me caged, but I was born to fly.* He was thinking, *Why can't she be more private? People are going to talk bad about her. Doesn't she understand the risks she's taking?* I know these were his thoughts because when I was finally brave enough to start "offending" him by actually having conversations and not just staying quiet about the things that bothered me, one day he said, "Baby, I admire you for what you do. You put yourself out there in front of everyone, and you're not scared about what they'll say, *but I am.* I see how mean people can be and what they say about others, and I don't want anyone talking bad about my baby."

Cue the tears. Hearing him say these words completely melted my heart. All his lashing out in the past over my work was his Critic identity. It had been leading the charge whenever it came to my dreams and providing a mask for his deep fears. This was the first time my husband had ever shown me this kind of emotional vulnerability. As Marines, we had been trained to keep it together, show no emotion, and focus on the mission. This was how my husband ensured his physical and emotional survival. Understanding where he was coming from really helped me have a new level of empathy for how endangered he felt whenever I stood onstage, gave an interview, or simply shared a vulnerable post on social media. This was a huge turning point for us.

It hasn't been easy—show me a marriage or a relationship worth keeping that is—but over the years we've created new dreams together. We both want the same things. We just want to take different paths to get there. I'm grateful that so far we've been able to run our own races on tracks that are close enough together that if either of us needs help, we can cross over and lend a helping hand before going back to our own lane. It may not work for everyone, but it works for *us*, for now. We'll revisit as needed and adjust accordingly. And *that*, my friend, is how you create a new possibility from giving yourself *permission to offend*.

PRINCIPLES OF OFFENDING WITH INTENTION

▶ Shying away and not being willing to offend in defense of your truth can be detrimental to your identity, mission, and purpose.

▶ It may be necessary to offend even in moments others might deem "inappropriate." Use judgment and wisdom to proceed accordingly.

▶ Although the observer of your truth might be offended, *your truth* is not offensive.

▶ For strategies to handle conversations, refer back to the nine core principles of offending with intention (page 193).

▶ Your body is capable of experiencing emotions before you're consciously aware of them. Practice checking in. Follow the steps listed in core principle 3 (page 194) or visit www.permissiontooffend .com/more for a guided scan audio.

▶ Review a person's body language, facial expression, and tonality to help ensure your intention is being accurately communicated.

> ❯ When you give yourself permission to offend, it might trigger the death of a dream someone had for your life. This is not your dream to resuscitate. Carry on in your truth.

───────── AFFIRMATION ─────────────────────────

I AM WILLING TO OFFEND IN SUPPORT OF MY TRUTH.

───────────────────────────── #PermissiontoOffend ─────────

At the end of the day, the best you can do is engage your Empathetic Offender identity and show up in truth—with love, care, empathy, and compassion. If you do all of that and others still think you're wrong, continue to work through the principles. Keep practicing. Be willing to "get it wrong." Consider the impact your truth will have on others. Whenever you feel it most appropriate for what you truly want in your life, *choose your dream* above the dreams others have for you.

We're coming to the end of our journey together. You're doing so good. Keep going. We're just about to get into the *mastery* level. I'll meet you there.

9

LIVE YOUR TRUTH

I failed. Worse than just failing, I failed *publicly*. I had made these huge statements on social media, declaring in faith, "We're going to have five hundred attendees at Confidence Activated! I know everyone says it's impossible, but I have faith. I believe it's possible."

Just between you and me, as I look back, I knew my goal was possible, but I didn't believe it was probable for *me*. Ever felt that way about something? You know a goal is possible, you even know it's probable for other people, but something inside you kind of doubts that it's possible *and* probable for you. Well, for as much as I wanted to believe and own the probability of achieving this goal, I didn't. I had never hosted an event of that scale. Some of my counterparts in the industry had a hundred grand to throw at an event and could handle the financial loss if things didn't work out. I didn't have that luxury. Every single penny I had was riding on this event. Literally: Every. Single. Cent.

As I walked into the main ballroom at the Whitley hotel in Atlanta, Georgia, my company was in the hole for $30,000, give or take a few pennies. We had put all the expenses on a credit card, and I was trusting God to perform a miracle. Not knowing what I didn't know, I had priced the tickets too low for what I wanted to deliver. As the date drew closer to the event, I could hear a voice echoing in my head. It was that of the girl who told me, "You can either give them an experience or you can make a profit—you can't do both." *Maybe she's right. Maybe I bit off more than I can chew. What the heck am I going to do? What if people don't show up? How am I going to pay for all of this?*

It wasn't just the money, although the weight of that financial burden was heavy. No, it was the fact that this new struggle was riding up on the backside of other failures after people had told me what I could and couldn't do. You see, about five or six years before my event I had begged my husband to take a chance on me and let me charge the first payment to his credit card—money we did not have—to become part of a mastermind group led by someone I deeply respected and admired. They had the house, the business, the family, the life many people, myself included, dreamed of one day having. I thought by joining this mastermind group and learning from them, I could have something similar.

At our first meeting, we were encouraged to go around the room and share what we were working on. I was so nervous. Everyone there except for me was already making multiple six figures and several were seven-figure earners. I felt lucky to be in the room, but also I felt inadequate. I *knew* I wasn't, but there was a small voice in my head telling me I didn't belong. When it was my turn, I took a deep breath and stood up. I turned my body to face both the leaders of the group on the platform stage as well as my colleagues around the tables. Nervously I began, "I'm Rachel Luna and I'm the Get Anything You Want Girl. . . . At least, that's what Tory Johnson from *Good Morning America* named me. But anyway, I help people get what they want. I have a twenty-one-day challenge called Get Anything You Want, and we've had great results. My next goal is to create an online course around confidence. I believe the number one thing holding people back from growing their business and getting more of what they want is their lack of confidence. My course can change that."

My heart was pounding as I eagerly looked around the room for approval. All my fears rushed to the surface, and I bit my lip to keep the tears from falling as my mentor callously said, "That's too vague. Get anything you want? No one is going to care about that. And twenty-one days is way too long. This whole confidence thing? That's also too vague. You need to niche down to something people care about."

I was stunned, embarrassed, and scared. *What if she's right? But I believe in this!* I argued with myself and then spoke up again, "But this is what my clients need. I've worked with them and surveyed them, and when our sessions are over, aside from making more money, the biggest result they get is a shift in confidence. I know this is what they need." I had tried not to be disrespectful, but I also wanted to be heard. More than anything, I wanted to be accepted and validated by my mentor.

Looking me in the eyes, my mentor proceeded to tell me, "Sell them what they want, give them what they need. They don't want confidence. They want something else." And that was that.

As I sat down in my chair—deflated and defeated—they proceeded to call on the next person. While the others took their turns around the room, all I could do was question all my decisions. *Have I gotten it all wrong?* I left the retreat feeling bummed but determined to prove myself. I thought being in the room and getting a seat at that table would be my opportunity to show others and myself that I was "worthy." I didn't realize it then, but I had attached my worth as a person to my financial net worth. Because I made less money than everyone else, I felt less than.

In the weeks that followed, I did my best to keep my head down and get to work. That is, until a couple of months later, when my mentor announced they were creating a course centered around—you guessed it—*confidence*. I was devastated. That might be an under-statement. Whatever is the ickiest feeling you can think of, that's what I felt. I mean, if we're being honest, and I am, I felt robbed. *They stole my idea!* That was my first thought. But who would believe me? They were the "A" players in my industry. They had the money, the power, the fame, the reputation. Who was I? No one. Nothing. It was my word against theirs, and even though others had been in the room when I'd spoken about my course, I knew no one would have my back. So I said nothing. Well, that's not true. I said a lot to my therapist. To everyone else, I kept my mouth shut. I didn't want to be the "negative" one in the group causing trouble.

The funny thing is that others in the group were having side conversations about how their expectations weren't being met, but no one was willing to speak up. I didn't understand why, if we were all so disappointed, everyone kept quiet. I mean, I knew why *I* kept my mouth shut. I was the least financially successful person in the group. Not to mention, I was the only brown girl. I didn't want to be perceived as the "loudmouth Latina," which is how I thought everyone already saw me anyway. But what about these rich white girls? Why weren't they speaking up?

The rich white girls had the exact same fears as I did. None of us wanted to get kicked out of the group. We all wanted to be accepted and validated by these industry leaders—so much so we were all will-ing to continue to make our monthly payments in this five-figure investment despite not actually receiving what we had been sold.

Another month or two went by, and I was feeling increasingly resentful toward my mentor. The company was full-force promot-ing their confidence program, and I still hadn't made any progress toward my own course. My biggest fear was that I would launch my program and people would accuse me of copying my mentor. My second biggest fear was that I would launch it and no one would buy it because they had already taken my mentor's course. Basically, I was letting someone else's decisions dictate how I moved in my own life. Major mistake.

What I know now that I didn't know then is that it doesn't matter. It doesn't matter if someone is already doing what you want to do—*do it anyway!* It doesn't matter if people think you're copying someone else. If you know deep in your heart of hearts that what you're creating is original, *let them talk!* No one can do what you do the way you do it. This was confirmed for me when I was given access to their confidence course and it was *nothing* like what I wanted to create. But I let my fears of being judged, rejected, and defamed hold me back.

Until one day, when it all came to a head. You know when you're in an environment that triggers you to no end and your central nervous system is shot and you dread showing up because you don't know if you're safe or if that might be the day you actually die? Okay, I'm being dramatic again, but seriously, that's how it *felt* sometimes when I would get on the group calls. I decided I needed to leave the mastermind group for my own mental health.

I made a call to one of the partners and said, "I'm so grateful for everything you've taught me up until this point, and I've decided that it's best for me to leave the group. I don't want a full refund because I have gotten value, but I would like a prorated refund since there are still several months left in the year." Speaking with this level of certainty took every bit of courage I had. At first, they were really kind. There was a lot of assurance that they were going to help me and suggested I take some time to think about it and then decide if I really wanted to walk away. We hung up the phone with me agreeing to think it over. I didn't really want to think it over, but they sounded so nice and caring on the call that I began to doubt myself. *Maybe I'm overreacting.*

A week or so later we were back on the phone, and I said, "I've thought it over, and again, I really appreciate everything you've taught me so far, but I think it's best for me to leave the group. Again, I don't want a full refund, but a prorated refund would be great." This time the voice on the other end wasn't as friendly. I could feel the anger as they said, "I thought we talked about this last week and I told you we'd help you." I explained that while I appreciated the offer, I was ready to move on. Mind you, what I really wanted to say was, "Help me? How? By stealing my idea and telling me no one cared about my work? Because if that's the kind of help you're offering, I'm good." But I didn't say that. I just listened as the voice on the other end got increasingly aggressive and defensive. They wanted specifics as to why I wanted to leave.

This was the part I had been dreading. *Do I speak my truth and tell them how I feel about their confidence program? What if they blacklist me in the industry? What if they say I'm crazy?* A million questions raced through my mind and I finally said, "Honestly? I was a little confused when you guys launched your confidence course because when I said at the retreat that I wanted to do a confidence course—" Before I could finish my sentence, I was cut off with a scoff: "Ha! Are you trying to say we took your idea? Oh boy! You are so lucky [partner's name] isn't on the phone with us because she'd really let you have it right now. She's been talking about confidence for years. We had already planned to do this."

My head was spinning. *Am I crazy? Maybe I'm overreacting. What if they've been planning this all along and I'm just being insecure? No! I have proof! This wasn't planned.* (I now know that what they were doing to me is called "*gaslighting,*" and they are lucky I wasn't then the woman I am today!)

I reminded myself that someone on their team had confessed to me that shortly after the retreat, my mentor and their team had gotten together and announced a new confidence course. Their team member had said, "It was a real push and they wanted it all done in, like, three weeks." I wasn't freaking crazy; these people were trying to play me! Now I was pissed. "Look, I'm not saying you stole my idea, but I think the timing is convenient, and when I said I was doing a confidence course, you never mentioned having one in the works." We went around the ring a few times, each taking small verbal jabs at the other. The call finally ended with an agreement to release me from my contract.

But that's not where the story ends. After the call, I followed up with an email to ensure there was a written request for my prorated refund. The reply shouldn't have surprised me, but it did. They were only willing to refund me a third of the prorated amount. Now, this *really* pissed me off. It was the final FU after everything they had done, and I wasn't having it. This time, the same old fears came up. *What if they blacklist me? What if they tell people I'm a bad person?* Blah, blah, blah, bullsh*t, bullsh*t, bullsh*t!

Nope! Not this time, Satan! I reached all the way into the depths of my truth, grabbed my ovaries, and wrote back the bravest email of my life up to that point. Regrettably, I have since deleted that email during my season of healing and forgiveness because life is too amazing to hold grudges. So I can't give you the word-for-word screenshot. But this was the gist of it:

"Thank you for your email. I have been a strong supporter of your business and would like to be able to continue to publicly speak positively about the work you do. The amount I am requesting is XXX."

I didn't know it then, but I was already developing the identity of an Empathetic Offender with that email. I spoke my truth. I was respectful. I had compassion for them while standing my ground. That's what this work is about, after all. Giving yourself permission to offend in support of what is most authentic to your values and beliefs.

They never responded to that email, but guess what they did. They gave me my money back almost immediately. Boom-shaka-laka for the win! And do you know *why* they gave me my money back? Because I gave myself allllllll the permission in the world to offend them. I was willing to risk my reputation in defense of my truth. I released my emotional attachment to the outcome and I surrendered. In the spirit of keeping it real, I'll admit it wasn't easy to get over the situation. But the more I've grown and integrated with my true identity, the less the actions and opinions of others trigger me. Oh, and by the way, about eighteen months later, I did end up launching a course around confidence. It was called the Confident Entrepreneur Academy, and in my first launch I generated over $52,000 in sales. This was a huge victory for me. I had a very small email contact list; Instagram was around, but I wasn't active on it; and I barely had followers on any of the other social media platforms.

With this new victory under my belt and a desire to learn how to scale it to the next level, I went in search of a new mentor. This next one, although very kind, caring, and genuinely wanting to see me win, *also* told me, "You can't sell confidence." Once again, I argued, "But I did it. I already sold confidence. My first launch was $52,000, and the second launch did almost $75,000. I'm already selling it." I wish I could tell you that I stood my ground and fought for my core promise: *The fastest way to build your business is to build your confidence.* I didn't. Instead, I retired the course and proceeded to create several other programs around sales, which was fine. I love and believe in the value of selling with integrity. It's just that, deep down, I wanted to work with people on their confidence and identity, not just their sales and marketing.

I stayed under this new mentor's guidance for two years, and I want to be clear: I got a tremendous amount of value from him and the mastermind group at large. But I didn't scale the way I wanted— not because of them but because *I never fully owned my truth.* I was successful to a degree. I grew my business to multiple six figures. I helped a lot of people along the way. But I struggled to feel truly aligned and always felt I was falling short of my full potential be-cause I wasn't living in my full truth. Remember that. You can only reach your full potential when you're living in your full truth.

Permission Slip

I give myself permission to live my full truth.

#PermissiontoOffend

As I share these stories with you, I'm reminded just how often people have wanted me to fit into their mold, to sell the way they sell, to speak the way they speak, to believe what they believe. Rather than lean into my true identity, or offend in support of my desires, I did my best to fit their mold.

I bet you can think of a few times when others have wanted you to bend and conform to accommodate their values, beliefs, and truths. I hope you can see that you don't have to live that way, and while there may be some consequences, the freedom you enjoy while living in your full truth will far outweigh the temporary pain you might experience.

It was a phone call from my friend Amber—who had been in that last mastermind group with me—that really helped me appreciate the pain of those experiences. As we were catching up, she said, with sincere pain in her voice, "Oh, Rachel, you've been shut down so many times. I remember watching you just sit there and take it. Everyone telling you that you couldn't do it. And now look at you. You're doing it!"

Even though I no longer needed validation, it was still nice to hear someone else confirm that I wasn't crazy. I *had* been shut down. I *had* been told my ideas weren't good. And I had overcome the op-position. By the time June 2019 rolled around, our final tally was 209 tickets sold for *Confidence Activated*. Maybe I didn't sell the 500 tickets that was my goal, but I sold an event based solely around the concept of *confidence*—the very thing the "celebrity" mentors in my industry had told me I couldn't do.

If this had been an exam, I would have scored a 41.8 percent—a big fat F! I thought I would be devastated, but in reality, all I could do was celebrate. That weekend, women from all over the world—yes, the world—lined up for registration! We had attendees from Canada, Barbados, and the United Kingdom as well as various states here in the US. The energy was electrifying. As a professional speaker, I've been on stages in front of thousands of people, and I can tell you, hand on my heart, the energy in that room of two hundred was just as powerful, if not more so, than rooms filled with triple the amount of people. I can only attribute that to God. To the power of intention. To the miracle of giving myself permission to offend, to execute a dream others might have considered a failure but I knew in my heart was something special. That's what that moment was for me.

Obviously I can't speak for every single attendee, but based on the feedback from those who completed our post-event survey, *we did our job and we did it well*! Lives were changed that weekend. Businesses were started, relationships were cultivated, and attendees made sales for their own businesses right in the room! And even though it was not a faith-based event, some who had previously experienced church hurt were able to restore their relationships with God. I may have gotten an F in ticket sales, but I most certainly got an A in transformation. I'll take that A any day! And the wins didn't stop there. That weekend my company generated over $90,000 in cash received. We made a profit of over $60,000 on the event *and* provided an incredible experience for our attendees.

Do not let anyone tell you something can't be done just because *they* can't do it.

Looking back, I think had we sold 500 tickets, my team and I might not have been able to provide such an incredible experience.

On staff, we had my husband; my best friend, Melisa; my assistant, Celita; Jenn, my marketing manager; and my integrator, Erica. We had five volunteers, and one attendee, Sandra, paid full price for a ticket, showed up, and then said, "I'm here to volunteer." Sandra donned a hot-pink "Activation Squad" volunteer shirt and worked her tail off for us all weekend—*even though she already had a paid seat in the room!*

Take a page from Sandra's book: find a need in the room and fill it. Because of Sandra's willingness to stand in the gap, not only did I end up hiring her on my team but also her servant's heart opened up opportunities to support several of my colleagues. That year, Sandra built her own six-figure business supporting other six- and seven-figure-earning entrepreneurs. I'm not saying she wouldn't have gone on to accomplish that on her own, but getting in the room and then being of high service most definitely accelerated her path.

Looking back, 209 was just the perfect number that weekend. That so-called ticket-sales failure has helped increase the level of gratitude and respect I have for all my other failures—the ones behind me and the ones yet to come. I thank failure for every lesson it provides. I'm grateful that failure has taught me that when we make statements of faith that don't manifest, it doesn't mean our faith isn't strong enough or that faith is dead. It means *nothing* except what we want it to mean. I've decided that when something I'm believing in doesn't manifest, it has less to do with my faith and more to do with my energy, beliefs, and actions. You can have faith and still doubt. I like to remind myself and others: you can be confident of the destination and still fear the journey. That was the next lesson I learned when, three days after the *Confidence Activated* event, I found the lump in my right breast that turned out to be an aggressive cancer. As I've shared, I had to give myself permission to offend over and over and over again in the weeks that followed. I was confident that my destination was going to be victory, but I sure was scared of the journey toward it. I'm so grateful we're here together now, a beautiful representation of the fact that victory was indeed inevitable.

Oh, and guess what? We hosted Confidence Activated *again* in 2021! We don't really have the time to go into the challenges I had to overcome just to get back into that room (you can listen to episodes 59 and 60 of the *Permission to Offend* podcast if you wanna know), but there's one thing I do want you to know right now. I used almost every lesson I've outlined in this book to help me give myself permission to offend and invite Jamie Kern Lima, a woman *Forbes* named one of "America's Richest Self-Made Women," to be our keynote speaker. Jamie founded It Cosmetics and went on to sell the company to L'Oréal for $1.2 billion (*yes, billion with a b*). In 2020 she became a *New York Times* bestselling author, and in 2021 she was the keynote speaker at Confidence Activated, an event that so many had told me I'd never be able to pull off.

I had absolutely no reason to believe that Jamie would say yes to me. At this time, she had already been speaking on stages with stadium-size audiences alongside Tony Robbins and others of similar prominence. I didn't have the budget to pay her speaking fee. I didn't have the clout or even the numbers to warrant inviting someone of her caliber to be our keynote speaker. Remember, I hadn't even hit my original goal of 500 tickets the first time around! But you know what I did have? *Faith!* I had faith, belief, and a vision for more! More for myself. More for my attendees. More for the event itself. I used a very simple method I'll teach you in just a bit. But just remember that it's safe for you to want, believe, and expect more!

CELEBRATED, NOT SHUNNED

A friend and I were talking about the women we love working with and the problems they often face when I said, "She wants to be celebrated, not shunned, for wanting more." My closest girlfriends, clients, students, and even the attendees of my live events have all expressed this same sentiment one way or another. *I want more and I don't want to feel bad about it.*

We want to be encouraged to want more. We don't want to be told we're selfish or to be questioned as to why we aren't happy with what we already have. We are! We are totally happy. Okay, well, maybe not *totally.* After all, I still don't have a live-in house manager who ensures my green juices are freshly pressed on the hour and fresh flowers are neatly arranged in each room of my house. One day, friend, one day. But seriously, can we give ourselves *permission* to want more without feeling guilt, shame, or selfishness? Let's normalize wanting more. Let's celebrate, not shun, ourselves and others for wanting more.

Permission Slip

I give myself permission to want more without feeling guilt, shame, or selfishness.

#PermissiontoOffend

It's time for you to make it okay to not only want more but also *say* and proudly *pursue* the things you want without regard for the comments from the peanut gallery. Imagine feeling excited about asking for a raise or raising your rates instead of agonizing about it and overthinking how others will react when you make your big ask. Imagine telling your friends and family about the exotic vacation you want to take without feeling like you need to downplay it so they don't get jealous. Imagine having candid conversations about your wildest dreams without fearing judgment, rejection, or defamation for wanting to experience something unimaginable to most.

Because—at least according to me—wanting more does not mean you're ungrateful. This is why it was so important in the very beginning of this book for us to talk about what we make things mean. Can you and I agree that wanting more doesn't mean we're not grateful, that instead it really just means that *we want more? Period?* Maybe it even means there's something else we're meant to do, to feel, to have, to experience. If that's what you make it mean, then that's what it means. If you've done the work laid out in this book, then you're hopefully at a point where, yeah, it's annoying when someone doesn't understand your vision. It's frustrating when people don't "get" your dreams. It's disappointing when others don't see what you're trying to do or why. But none of that stops you. You get to want, pursue, and have more! That's the gift of giving yourself permission to offend and living unfiltered, unashamed, and unafraid.

I can't speak for you; I can only speak for myself. But when I think of everything I have and where I came from, wow—I'm beyond grateful. I wish I could say I never thought I'd be here, but the reality is, I did. I didn't just think I'd be here. I *knew* I'd be here. Even during the times when it didn't look like things were going to happen for me, there was still a knowing inside me. It was *the knowing* that kept me moving forward. I think you have that knowing too, and that's why you were led to this book.

And guess what? There's another level waiting, not just for me but also *for you.*

Even though I am perfectly content and supremely grateful for all I have right in this moment, I know God's not done with me yet. The next level you and I have been called to—the one that others may judge, reject, and/or possibly even defame—is the very one that paves the path for someone else. Because as the little girl who was born to HIV-infected parents, whose father was a high-functioning, drug-abusing alcoholic—a girl who endured abuse, disordered eating, promiscuity, and other trauma—I should have been a statistic. But I'm not. Because I made it this far, I know I've already given so much hope to others. It's this knowing that, especially on really tough days, allows me to imagine how much hope and inspiration my next level will give to other little girls. I beam with excitement when I envision having my first seven-figure-earning year and the encouragement it will bring to other women over forty who wonder if it's ever going to happen for them. (Spoiler alert: *Yes!* It's happening for me and for *you!*)

As soon as you give yourself permission to offend, *you*, my dear friend, will be the one who gives everyone watching you permission to do the same. Wouldn't it be amazing if we all lived in that freedom? *You* have the power and all the tools available to you right now to be the one who starts a legacy for her family.

LEANING INTO SELF-INTEGRITY

When I was in the Marine Corps, I was taught in boot camp that the definition of "integrity" was doing the right thing when no one was around to see you do wrong. It's an external expression of your intentions. On the other hand, self-integrity is internally focused. "Self-integrity" means keeping your word to yourself. It's staying true to what you value and believe. It's doing the things you said you'd do *before* you say yes to doing the things others ask of you. The higher your level of self-integrity, the more confident you become. When you're confident in who you are, what you want, and where you're headed, you begin to care less about the opinions and judgments of others. As we've already covered, it doesn't mean you *never* think about what others might think. It's just that now it doesn't stop you from doing and saying the things you want.

One reason so many people struggle with taking action is because they suffer from low self-integrity. Boundaries have been breached and promises made to oneself have been broken. This constant self-betrayal has formed a pattern, and the only way to change the pattern is to create a new neural pathway in the brain. My favorite way (because it's the easiest and I like easy things) is going to sound so basic. I mean, truly *it is*—but it works! People don't give enough credit to the basics. But think of a delicious loaf of warm, crusty, doughy bread. What's it made of? Four *basic* ingredients. Almost all bread starts with just flour, water, yeast, and salt. Once you know how to make a basic loaf, then you can start getting all fancy-schmancy. So here we go: the basic strategy to help you increase your self-integrity, create a new neural pathway, and experience transformation is to create a pattern of quick wins. Choose something that is *so* simple, it'll be impossible for you not to stick with it for three days. I'm talking *eeeaaaaasssssyyyyyy*. Something like taking one multivitamin in the morning with your cup of coffee. (Pro tip: Set your multivitamin bottle right next to your coffee maker and boom! Nailed it.) Another simple thing to do might be to make your bed as soon as you wake up.

Your mission is to set a ridiculously simple goal for yourself that you can achieve three days in a row. Each day that you achieve the goal, *celebrate it!* I'm talking big-time celebration. Treat yourself to something fun, indulge in a movie, savor a delicious piece of chocolate, unplug from work, or go for a long stroll. The celebration part is key. This is a step most people skip and then they wonder why they aren't seeing results. If you don't celebrate the victory, then the reward centers in your brain aren't activated, and as such, you won't develop the pathway of victory.

Once you've completed this three-day challenge, you're on your way to developing higher levels of self-integrity. Likewise, I strongly recommend you do something celebratory whenever you set and honor boundaries with yourself and others.

ALIGNMENT OPPORTUNITY

Use this space to map out your three-day Self-Integrity Challenge.

What's one easy thing you can do every day for the next three days? (Example: write one thing I'm grateful for each morning.)

What can you do to stack this action with something you already do every day? (Example: place my journal on my nightstand next to my phone so my hand touches the journal before it touches the phone.)

Write down how you will celebrate, and remember to make a big deal so your brain gets the memo that you're winning! (Example: have a morning dance party with my family.)

Bonus: *After the three days are up, journal your thoughts around how it felt to complete these three days. What came up for you? Where did you experience resistance? How was your self-integrity challenged?*

We discussed boundaries in chapter 5, and as you move on to embody the identity of the Empathetic Offender, you're going to need strong boundaries so you can stand up, speak out, and live in truth, faith, and freedom. This can be as simple as a quick check-in, but I recommend, especially in the beginning, you set some intentional time to get clear every day. I wasn't kidding when I said transformation requires daily dedication. Not taking action doesn't keep things the same; it makes them worse.

Consider this: A dear friend gifts you a stunning plant. It's beautifully potted in a gorgeous stone holder. The leaves are vibrant; the soil looks lush and fertile. You place the plant on a window that gets just the right amount of light. Each day you walk by the plant, noticing its beauty but never stopping to give it water or to dust its leaves. What happens to the plant? Does it continue to flourish and grow? Does it stay the same? You might not notice it at first. It may even take weeks or months before you realize the plant has started to wither and needs attention. If you continue to leave it where it is, not doing anything at all, it won't flourish. Nor will it remain the same. It will simply die a slow death.

If you want the results I've promised you from this book, it's going to take more than just reading it from cover to cover and then placing it on your bookshelf. The real work begins once you start going about your day-to-day business. Will you be mindful to hydrate your mind and dust the leaves of your soul?

Here are some questions to journal around to help you stay mentally hydrated, increase your self-integrity, *and* enforce your boundaries:

TAKE INVENTORY

What are my goals?

What do I value?

What do I believe?

What do I stand for and against?

Answering these questions regularly, if not daily, is critical. We live in a world where we're drowning in information but thirsty for wisdom. The best way to begin to sift through the thousands of data points you're consuming each day is to first be rooted in *your* truth. Otherwise, what's the point of giving yourself permission to offend?

Fun fact: research has shown that people who write their goals down every day are more likely to achieve them. I hated doing this.

I don't even want to admit it, but I'm gonna because I think this might help someone. Sometimes I *still* struggle to write down my goals every day, because it scares me! There. I said it. Writing down my goals every day scares me. I push myself to do it, though, because it holds me so accountable that I can't use any excuses to not take action.

Beyond writing down my goals, I have a strong journal practice to support me. If you're not "the journaling type," I highly recommend you give yourself permission to work on your beliefs and values around writing. It's one of the most powerful tools I could ever recommend, and that's not just my personal experience. I've seen how journaling has completely shaped and changed lives for hundreds of my clients.

ASSESS

At the end of each day, use the following questions to assess how you showed up in the world. Relax—you don't have to answer them *all* every single day. I'm giving you options. Choose one or two and get connected to yourself:

Did I speak my truth today?

When, if at all, did I hold back?

How did speaking up or holding back help me get closer to my goals?

Who needed my voice today?

Did my actions align with the identity I desire to embody?

Am I proud of the person I was today in front of and behind closed doors?

Let's be clear: These assessment questions aren't meant for you to beat yourself up over what you did or did not do. They are simply methods in which to hold yourself accountable. You're on a mission to make your mark in this world, and as such, you're being called to higher levels of accountability. If you are going to be someone out here offending people in these streets, then you better get accountable to yourself first before you try to hold someone else accountable.

ACKNOWLEDGE

Being honest with yourself about your energy level, your emotional well-being, and any nonnegotiable commitments already scheduled is another way to stay accountable and maintain high levels of self-integrity.

> *How's my energy today?*
>
> *What would energize me?*
>
> *What activities will drain my energy today?*
>
> *What are my nonnegotiable commitments for today?*
>
> *What would excite me?*

On any given day, my rule of thumb is no more than three needle-moving activities per day. This is because I *know* myself. Attention deficit disorder is real. Despite the wonderful all-natural supplements I take to assist me, it's still a gift I get to work with, and some days it's more challenging than others.

Know yourself. You don't have to change *everything* about who you are. You just have to be honest about where you are right now and continue to walk in the direction of your dreams with compassion and empathy for yourself as well as for others. That's where the freedom resides.

THREE STEPS TO MANIFESTING FREEDOM (AND ANYTHING ELSE YOU WANT)

I literally just eye-rolled as I typed the word "manifesting." Mainly because, in my opinion, it's been so wildly overused that people have forgotten what it really means. Manifesting isn't about magic or conjuring up some mystical entity to grant you the desires of your heart. Rather, the literal dictionary definitions of "manifest" include:

> *Display or show (a quality or feeling) by one's acts or appearance; demonstrate.*
>
> *Be evidence of; prove.*
>
> *Become apparent through the appearance of symptoms.*

When you and I talk about manifesting something, we're talking about doing the work necessary to show, prove, and make something appear—in this case, your dreams, desires, and ultimately freedom. There are several ways to manifest your desires, just like there are many different paths to take from one corner of the world to another. This is *my* way. Try it on for size. If you don't love it, that's fine. You won't offend me. ☺

I call this the Faith Activated Journaling Method. This is the exact method I've used to help thousands of people—friends, family, clients, students, podcast listeners, members of my Faith Activated Journaling Experience—bring more of their desires to life. Those who have used this method have been able to manifest things like:

- Medical bills forgiven
- New cars purchased
- Marriages saved from divorce
- Children's behavior improved
- Job promotions offered
- Health transformed
- Vision clarified
- Goals achieved
- Relationships cultivated

Your reading this book is a result of me using the Faith Activated Journaling Method. I followed the method to manifest my agent, HarperOne as my desired publishing house, and even the amount of my book advance! Using the Faith Activated Journaling Method (plus a little help from God) is exactly how I was able to get Jamie Kern Lima to speak at Confidence Activated. (P.S. If you have a strong negative association with the word "journaling," then call it "writing"—whatever helps you take action and gets you excited to try it.)

Okay, here we go. It's super simple: *write, shift, script.* That's it!

WRITE

WRITE WHATEVER COMES UP FOR YOU. Literally *anything.* Here's an example of how one of my own journal entries began:

> *Good morning! I'm kind of dragging. I almost lost the fight with my bed, but I managed to escape and get out of the house. This month is flying by and I think/feel that I haven't done any of the things I thought I would do by this time, this month. Ugh! And on top of that, I got an*

email this morning basically rejecting my pitch. Not only did they not accept my pitch, but they didn't even try to counter!

All I can think is a victim story: "Why not me?" Why does Marisa get brand deals to pay her tens of thousands of dollars and I get scrap?

Bleh! I know these questions aren't the best questions to ask myself. I know they don't help. But it's all I can hear in my head. Oh great! Now my face is leaking and I'm in front of all these people at this coffee shop. I need to get it together, but all these negative thoughts keep invading my mind.

What am I making this rejection mean?

Notice how the beginning of this entry is just a bunch of nothing? Then I go into everything that's on my mind to include words like "ugh!" And "bleh." I'm super honest and vulnerable, sharing even the parts that I don't want to admit. That's the process. Please do not overthink this step. The only way you can mess this up is by trying to edit yourself. Be willing to answer whatever questions naturally come up. Let your truest thoughts run onto your paper. Okay. Let's continue.

SHIFT

SHIFT INTO A STATE OF GRATITUDE AND EXPECTATION. Gratitude and love are the highest-frequency emotions we can experience. By shifting into a high-frequency vibration, we open up our capacity to manifest. I encourage you to also feel the energy of expectations, because when you expect your desires to come true, you get excited about them. And actions that are fueled by excitement tend to bring more joy and fulfillment. When you practice gratitude, your brain releases dopamine and serotonin. Dopamine helps you take action

toward your goals. If that's not enough to get you practicing gratitude, maybe it will help you to know that researchers at the University of Oregon found that journaling gratitude increases generosity
(a bonus for everyone in your world!).*

Here's how I shifted in that same journal entry used previously:

> *Thank you, Lord. It is such a gift and treasure to be in this space
> and environment. Thank you for moments of rejection and for
> reminding me that every rejection is simply a redirection. Thank you
> for every opportunity I've ever had that's led me to this moment and
> thank you for all the opportunities that are waiting for me up ahead.
> Thank you that people of influence are working on my behalf. Thank
> you that people of influence are conspiring for my greatest and
> highest good.*

Side note: Most of my journal entries, even in the *Write* step,
begin with me praising God, but if that's not your cup of tea, that's
fine. Here's an example of the *Shift* step from another entry:

> *I love the idea of POSSIBILITIES and playing in the space of what's
> possible and "Wouldn't it be amazing if . . . ?" That feels so good and
> exciting. I feel all buzzy just thinking of how many things are available
> and possible for me and my family.*
>
> *Today I'm so excited about the idea of Bella and Nina loving
> veggies, fruits, moving their bodies, and living an organic-plant-
> based life. I love the idea that my daughters live an incredibly
> joyful, fulfilled life.*

---

* Christina M. Karns, William E. Moore III, and Ulrich Mayr, "The Cultivation
of Pure Altruism via Gratitude: A Functional MRI Study of Change with Gratitude
Practice," *Frontiers in Human Neuroscience*, December 12, 2017, https://www.frontiersin
.org/articles/10.3389/fnhum.2017.00599/full.

In this example you can see I'm not necessarily talking about gratitude but about excitement and possibility. These are things that light me up. When you do the *Shift* step, focus on writing something that gets you primed for goodness.

SCRIPT

SCRIPT YOUR DESIRES AS IF THEY ALREADY ARE. This step is my favorite! If you do nothing else, please do this step! The objective is to write what you want in the present tense as if it's your current reality. Brain scans have shown that how our brain reacts to real life isn't very different from how it reacts to something we're imagining.

Here's the *Script* step that immediately followed my second example in the *Shift* step:

> I'm so happy and excited that Bella and Nina are happy, they are living their dreams, they are self-assured, confident, and secure in their identities. My daughters love the Lord. They spend time reading the Bible every day. They are best friends. They are avid readers. They care about making the world a better place. They know how to separate the facts from their stories. Above all, my daughters are happy.

When I wrote that entry in October 2019, I was three months in remission and I had drastically changed my diet to an all-organic vegan lifestyle, following the Gerson Therapy. While I was dining on oil-free, salt-free, nut-free, dairy-free, gluten-free, mostly flavor-free food, my family was still living it up on salty, oily, carnivorous fare. I wish I could proudly say that at least the food they were eating consisted of traditional Puerto Rican delights like *arroz con gandules*, *pernil*, and *plátanos maduros*. But no, the standard diet in our home heavily relied on Publix grocery store fried chicken, pizza, and Kraft macaroni and cheese. If I so much as offered a leaf of lettuce or a slice of fruit to accompany the meals, it was a full-on battle.

Knowing that the cancer I had developed wasn't predicated on genetics, my belief was that environment, stress, and diet were the major contributors to the diagnosis. As a wife and mother, I wanted to do everything I could to protect my family. Since talking to my little crew wasn't moving the needle, I turned to my journal and thought, *Why not? I have nothing to lose and everything to gain.* I should also mention that while I love God and am frequently blasting praise music at volume one thousand, my daughters, especially my youngest, had never really seemed that interested. Whenever I invited them to pray or have Bible study with me, it was eye-roll city. So I added that script in there for good measure as well.

Fast-forward to today. While my family is still feasting on their usual Standard American Diet, they also now add fruits, carrot sticks, cucumbers, and the occasional leaf of lettuce to their plates. We pray together every morning during our drive to school, with my girls usually taking turns leading, and finally, they're really getting along and have formed the sisterly bond I had always hoped they'd have. Make no mistake: this wasn't just a one-time journal entry, click my heels together, and poof everything I had dreamed of was manifested into reality. Not at all. The reason this method worked is because it coupled faith with *action*.

Writing your truth, aligning with gratitude and then scripting your desires as if they've already come to life is the activation of your faith. It takes faith to see and hold a vision. It takes faith to write it down with full expectation. It takes faith to declare a thing done.

Because of the way the mind functions, as you write things down in your journal, your subconscious gets to work, looking for the evidence of what you've written. The more you ignite self-integrity and honor your boundaries, the more you begin to achieve. Take time to *take inventory, assess,* and *acknowledge* yourself each day and combine that with the Faith Activated Journaling Method. This will give you tangible action steps that go hand in hand with your faith. The Bible says, "Faith without works is dead" (James 2:26, NKJV). These steps help you do both.

Your turn: Choose a goal, dream, or desire you'd like to manifest. Write it down so you have it at the top of your mind.

GOAL: _____

If it's easier, here's a prompt for you: *What do I want to manifest this year?*

(Some of the members of my Faith Activated Journaling Experience have reported it's easier for them to get started when I offer a prompt in the form of a question.)

WRITE:

SHIFT:

SCRIPT:

I've included additional journal prompts in the back of the book to help you jump-start your practice.

Here's an example of the *Write* step of the Faith Activated Journaling Method from one of our members.

Prompt: Whose opinions do I need to stop obsessing over?

WRITE.

Hmm. Such a good question! Definitely need to stop obsessing over what "others" think of me. Who are these "others?" Actually having to think about this ... the people I obsess about are probably not even caring that much. It's the "watchers," the people who are just sitting back + not engaging with the content ... honestly why am I caring so much about their opinion?

Oh, I think it's because I want to be liked by everyone. I think I still have that part of me that wants the approval of my parents + I project it on everyone else.

SHIFT.

Wow, thank you God for bringing that to the forefront ... again! I know that you bring this up to remind me that the only opinion that matters is your opinion of me + I know you love me unconditionally + while I know you desire the greatness in me to come up fully + greatness is my portion, I know you do not judge me or need anything from me to be loved by you.

SCRIPT.

It's amazing what freedom comes when I've stopped obsessing about the "views" + "likes" on social media. I feel so empowered to just show up authentically as me + speak my truth. And you know what? The response has been phenomenal as well. The DMs to work with me have started coming in + my calendar is now booked up with coaching clients + the revenue is now rolling in! Praise God + yay for freedom from the opinion of "others." I'm already approved by God!

WHY THIS WORKS

As I mentioned earlier, this practice isn't about magic or anything that suggests all you have to do is write something down and boom, a miracle happens! I'm not saying that's not possible. Far be it from me to minimize your faith. I'm saying this method will help you get primed and open to new possibilities. It's about allowing yourself to welcome and receive more of what you desire.

Our brains are activated when we write down what we desire as if it's already become a reality. You may not realize it consciously, but your mind will begin to look for more of what you wrote down in your journal in your everyday life. For example, when I originally wrote down that my daughters were best friends, in reality they were often fighting with each other, throwing each other under the bus, and generally treating each other pretty cruelly. Because I was so committed to helping them change their relationship, and I often journaled about it, in retrospect I can see how in that season many of our conversations began to center around the importance of sisterhood. Before my journaling, I had not really talked about the values and benefits of being both sisters and friends.

Likewise, because I was journaling around helping my children expand their palates, I found myself looking for images, recipes, and activities that would get them excited about trying new foods. When you write down a vision and make it plain, your mind wants to help you bring it to life. The more you focus on what you desire—as if it's already happened—the more you're able to take steps toward having it all.

Speaking of having it all, if you're still feeling hesitation or doubt around journaling, take a look at chapter 11, where I've included some journal examples from skeptics who gave it a try and have manifested things they never thought possible. What will you lose by trying? I hope you've learned from my failures that nothing is ever truly lost; everything is a lesson learned. Sometimes it's a lesson we need to learn more than once.

A SEAT AT THE TABLE

As we approach the final stop on our journey together, I want to make sure I answer some final questions. How can you walk in freedom if the rest of the world hasn't yet caught up on this whole *Permission to Offend* framework? What does it look like to combine all the work you've been accomplishing throughout this book and apply it in such a way that you are able to wake up each day ready to make your mark, unfiltered, unashamed, and unafraid?

The answer to both questions is simple: *practice*. One thing I've learned in doing this work myself is that living freely doesn't mean living without challenge or opposition. There will *always* be someone who has something to say. I know this to be true because I spent many months poring over reviews and testimonials of books, products, services, even Michelin-star restaurants in an attempt to make a case that maybe, just maybe, there's a way to create something that no one can find fault with. Sadly, I couldn't find even *one* completely positive review for anything. Granted, I didn't research everything on the market, but, legit, I put in some serious hours. It was something I had to do to silence the little voice in my head that wanted me to create something that would please everyone. Personally, I can't, and knowing that I won't ever be able to is really comforting. It kind of takes the pressure off.

You're gonna get it wrong. You're gonna mess up. One day your courage to speak up will result in the wrong choice of words, or body language or facial expression or tonality. Or maybe even the actual belief you hold won't be well received. I don't know about you, but I can't live my life obsessing over that day. Instead, choose to embody the Empathetic Offender identity and continue to work on the nine core principles we covered in chapter 8 to the best of your ability. When I do this, the reward of embodying this work is beyond anything I can express in words. Receiving emails and messages from people thanking me for saying what they were thinking and telling me how sharing my truth has helped them own their truth, that right there is priceless.

What if by sharing *your* truth you discover that not only have you helped someone through a rough moment but also you have actually helped save a marriage or *a life*?! That's been my reality, but only after I gave myself permission to offend. Prior to that, I was often told I was "so inspiring" or "so motivating," but little or no action was being taken by these people. The braver I have become on this journey, the braver those in my world have become. Together we have stood up and spoken out against the injustices we've seen in this world. We're starting to see that not only are *real* conversations being had but also actual accountability is taking place. We're not willing to sit idly by as oppression and fake diversity are marketed. Our voices and platforms are being used to educate, instigate, and activate. I'm just gonna keep it real and tell you—that I'm a woman of color who was never quite sure where she fit in. Now I get to say, "I fit in wherever I want to fit in!"

It's been almost a decade since I had that experience with my first mastermind group mentor, and in that time, I've seen her on several occasions at different events. Each time we've been cordial and professional. I hold no grudges. If anything, *I'm grateful*. As I reflect on that experience, it was the inception of me learning how to honor *my* truth. It was the first time I had to walk in high faith where my business was concerned, which then gave me the confidence to keep walking in faith in other areas of my life. Hand to God, I have nothing but deep appreciation for that mastermind group and for who I was then. I didn't know it then, but that experience was exactly what

I needed to help shape who I am today. From the depths of my soul, I'm so grateful to them, to myself, and to the challenges of that season. It's what led me to develop these frameworks and strategies over the years. It's what has led you and me to be here together.

Doing this work has helped me and so many others discover that the coveted seats at the tables we once thought we wanted to dine at are actually filled with people we don't even want to associate with. As a result, we are now setting our own tables, and the guest list is *almost* all-inclusive. Our sole requirement is that when you join us, you do so in the full embodiment of your Empathetic Offender identity. Come all who are empathetic, patient, compassionate, loving, and understanding. Your opinions are welcome. Your truth is heard. Should we disagree, we'll do so with a commitment to seeking understanding and a mutual respect for the belief that two truths can coexist. If for some reason we can't, then we each retreat to our homes with the knowledge that there is still work to be done.

The reality is that transformation requires frequent—most often *daily*—application. Be daring. Enforce boundaries. Set yourself up for rejection. Come back to the book often, and choose a principle to apply regularly.

After you eventually close this book, remember that when you live your truth and give yourself *permission to offend*, you get to have it all.

You. Get. To. Have. It. All.

PART 4

I GIVE MYSELF PERMISSION TO LIVE IN ABUNDANCE

May the Lord, the God of your ancestors, increase you a thousand times and bless you as He promised you.

—DEUTERONOMY 1:11, NIV

Congratulations! You get to have *more*. More truth, more faith, more freedom. You've made it to what might otherwise be considered an "appendix," but I refer to it as the abundance of this book. The journey isn't over just yet. In this section you'll find some key phrases to help enrich your empathetic vocabulary. These templates will come in handy as you start owning your truth and using your voice for change. I've also included case studies of how others have given themselves permission to offend and are now living more unfiltered, unashamed, and unafraid.

As you enter this final section of the book, I hope you remember that life is abundant and you are supported.

10

THE LANGUAGE
OF EMPATHY

Giving yourself *permission to offend* means you'll be activating your empathetic abilities, which at times can be quite exhausting if you're not prepared. For this reason, I want to give you some key phrases and tools to help you stay energized and empowered.

COMMUNICATING INTENT

"My intention is _____. And I hope the impact and effect it has on you and others will be _____ _____."

"I'm frustrated with _____, and by sharing my personal truth, my intention is to _____ _____."

"_____ is a cause I'm really passionate about. As I begin to share more, I hope you know my intention is to _____, and the impact I

hope it will have is _____."

ENROLLING IN THE VISION

"I've decided to _____, and it's

important to me because _____."

"I know this may seem out of character for me, and I really appreciate your support as I start to take actions that are more aligned with who I'm choosing to be moving forward."

"Thanks for taking the time to meet with me. I'm really excited about some new decisions I've made and I wanted to share them with you. It means a lot to me to know you're on my side."

"I'm so glad we have this chance to connect. Things are shifting for me, and I wanted to make sure I communicated with you so you're not surprised when you see what's up ahead for me."

SETTING BOUNDARIES

"I'm making some adjustments to my schedule and wanted to keep you updated. Of course I am still here for you, and these are the days/times when I can be most present. Thanks for honoring this."

"I care about you and want to be able to continue our relationship. It makes me uncomfortable when _____

happens." (Try not to assign blame. Call out the behavior, not the person.)

"I'm very uncomfortable when _____.
Moving forward, I would appreciate your help in making sure this doesn't continue."

"My business hours are _____. You can expect a response from me _____. Thank you for your patience and for respecting these guidelines."

ACKNOWLEDGING THE OTHER PERSON'S EMOTIONS

You've done it! You have embodied your Empathetic Offender and spoken your personal truth with high faith. Now the other person is having a strong reaction. Here are some statements and questions you can offer up to get to a place of understanding:

"I can see you're upset, and I understand how frustrated you feel right now. I'm available to listen and answer any questions you have."

"I'm sorry you're hurting. It's okay to be upset."

"It's okay to cry and express your feelings. I'm here to listen."

"I understand where you're coming from. I'm sorry we don't agree. I'm committed to working through this with you."

"I know this is hard for you to accept. Thank you for hearing me out."

"I care about you. Please take all the time you need to process. I'll be here when you're ready to talk and reconnect."

"I am sorry. Please give me grace. I would like some time to think and be thoughtful in my response."

"I want to give you a loving, thoughtful response. I don't want to react defensively or minimize your feelings."

"Are you willing to give me some time to really think about what I've done and/or said so that we can come to an understanding?"

"I know you prefer to process things right in the moment and talk through every little detail. I'm willing to do that with you after I've had some time to get my thoughts together."

"I want to make sure you understand why I'm not ready to talk just yet. It has nothing to do with you. This is who I am and how I process. I need some time to myself. It doesn't mean (insert whatever story you believe they have). I care about you, and because I care, I want to be thoughtful, intentional, and respectful when we speak."

"I would like X amount of time to think and process. Let's have lunch (give a specific date and time). I really appreciate your support in this."

"I'm available for dialogue. Let's discuss this."

"You've mentioned I didn't celebrate your achievements and that hurt you. What can I do next time to help you feel more loved, honored, and celebrated?"

11

FAITH IN ACTION

As promised in chapter 9, I want you to be equipped with examples of how others have used the Faith Activated Journaling Method to manifest incredible results on their terms. I'll be sure to point out the *Write*, *Shift*, and *Script* of each example so that you can see exactly how this works "in the wild." You'll also find seven days of journal prompts to give this method a try.

I hope you give yourself permission to get out of your comfort zone and try this journaling method. I know that if you stick with it, like so many others who have made this practice part of their lifestyle, you will see a beautiful transformation.

THE FAITH ACTIVATED JOURNAL METHOD "IN THE WILD"

THE WORST YEAR BECAME THE BEST

I received an email from Javacia, a member of my Faith Activated Journaling Experience and she had written this:

> Hi, Rachel,
>
> I'm not sure if this is too meta, but my most powerful manifestation was about Faith Activated. I joined FA when I was about to start chemo and I journaled that journaling would help me thrive in spite of chemo, and it did!
>
> An excerpt from my journal entry is attached.
>
> I wrote this right after I joined FA. Everything in this entry came true. After journaling, to receive the manifestation I committed to not living like a sick person. I kept writing and working and walking every day for exercise. And I kept journaling. And it worked!

Let's take a look at Javacia's journal entry together. It's a great example to help illustrate an important note about The Faith Activated Journal Method. The method is *cyclical* not linear. That means that you don't always have to go in order. I teach it in the *Write, Shift, Script* order to make it easy to follow and remember.

Notice that in this example, Javacia skips the *Shift* step of the method and goes straight from the *Write* to the *Script*.

> WRITE. 2020 could have been the worst year of my life. And at first, I thought it would be. On January 24 I was diagnosed with breast cancer. Then COVID-19 sent the world into a global health pandemic and economic crisis.
>
> SCRIPT. But I began a new journaling practice—one fueled by faith—and I began to trust and rely on God like never before.

As a result, I not only survived COVID, cancer, and chemotherapy—I thrived.

During my chemotherapy and radiation treatments, I was so healthy physically, mentally, emotionally, financially, and spiritually that people around me saw this as a miracle. They knew this was the work of God and grew closer to God because of my testimony and my story.

Instead of chemo brain, I got chemo creativity! Throughout my treatments, I had a flood of ideas for building my business and for essays and stories and God gave me the strength to bring them to fruition. And I made the most lucrative year ever in spite of all the obstacles.

As I read her journal entry I couldn't help but feel moved almost to tears. She activated her faith, used her journal to help decide what her experience would be, and she thrived!

To be clear: journaling is NOT a replacement for medical treatment and I am in no way saying or suggesting that journaling is a cure for cancer. But I do believe that journaling can support a person in their healing journey and this entry is an example of that.

WHOLEHEARTED BELIEF

This next example comes from a post shared in the "manifesting-momentum" channel in our Faith Activated Journaling community by Erica A. She wrote,

"Ya'll!!!! I wrote this THIS MORNING! This prompt brought a friend's name to my mind out of the blue, so I messaged her after journaling. We hopped on a call . . . and now I HIRED MY FIRST TEAM MEMBER!!!!! Talk about a QUICK manifestation!!!

Please note: the last script session was written HOURS before anything actually happened! I am ELATED and no longer surprised

when I journal, take the inspired action that comes from it, and
MANIFEST what's meant for me! #grateful

Can you tell she was excited? I have to tell ya, even though I read posts like this every single day from our members, I'm still always in awe at how powerful this practice can be. Let's take a look at her journal entry and just like before, I'll point out the steps in action.

The journal prompt: If I wholeheartedly believe without a doubt that
I already have enough and what I want is 100 percent available to me,
what would I do today?

WRITE. I would hire for my abilities—tech and admin. I keep thinking
about Krysta. She would be such a great admin/partner! I really want
to grow a team and know that will also allow me to grow as a leader.
When I have support in place, I would also join Maya's program. I know
I would rock it and learn so much!

SHIFT. I am so ready to commit to posting! I have things to say.
Stories are evidence.

SCRIPT. Wow! I did it! I did it! I hired my first team member! She
is incredible and totally what I dreamt of and more! We had our first
team meeting and I choked back tears of gratitude! We are going to
kick so much ass together! I feel even more excited and prepared for
exponential growth! Thank you, Jesus!

Do you wanna know why I think Erica A. was able to experience such a quick manifestation? It's because deep down this was something she already wanted and all she needed was to unlock a little more personal faith and belief in herself. Once she journaled and scripted a new, possible reality, her subconscious mind got to work, looking for proof in her waking life to confirm her vision.

Of course, she also had to take action! After journaling she didn't just sit on her hands. Nope. She sprang into action, reached out to her friend, got on a call, and made the ask. Can you see how this method isn't "magic"? It's a tool to help you get more clarity, increase your faith, and belief in yourself and take faster action.

Let's look at one more.

ALL OUR DREAMS ARE COMING TRUE

This final example is from Taryn. Taryn is a single mom who has really gone through some hard times. When she joined our community she and her son were living with family as Taryn did her best to get back on her feet. When she posted this in our "manifesting-momentum" channel we all cheered and celebrated with her. Here's what she wrote:

> *Manifestation alert!!!*
>
> *I brought my game face this week because I have some big goals—things that have logistically not been possible before this week but that I want and need to lean into and manifest . . .*
>
> *I wrote the two things I wanted to manifest this week . . . neither of which I could really see how they would come to pass, but both of which are a part of my bigger mission this month/year.*
>
> *I kept taking the action that I had control over—just my little part . . . and I journaled . . . and I shifted in my mindset to feel what it would feel like to be the type of woman who has these things come to pass in her life.*
>
> *One of the things is to get approved on my own, no cosigner, for a car loan this week. I'm blessed to have a car currently that runs, but it's on its last legs for being safe for me and my son.*
>
> *I had applied before, and because I've been a stay-at-home mom in prior years, I didn't make enough on my own to get approved.*
>
> *Business has gone well this past year, thanks to God and all the favor He has given me . . . so I applied for the loan last week to see.*

There was a bunch of red tape that I thought for sure would throw away any chance I had: I work for myself, so no W2s or traditional pay stubs, my business wasn't up and running properly until 2021 so I didn't have tax info to prove income, etc....

The next day, I checked my email.

The loan officer I had applied with emailed me and said I'd been approved—not for the small amount I had originally asked for ... but enough for a brand new car. A 2022. New. Car. At a massively low rate ...

I'm not crying—you're crying. 😂

I manifested a house last month in the same way ... I did my part, journaled around it, and God made a way where there was no way. I'm sitting in my NEW office in my new house, with tears of gratitude for my new car that awaits me.

Thank you, Rachel Luna. All my dreams are coming true with YOU in 2022!

At the start of that year I had shared an affirmation with the group: "All our dreams are coming true in 2022!" Although I thought it was sweet of Taryn to thank me, the truth is: she did the work!

Here's the journal entry that helped generate Taryn's manifestations:

The journal prompt: What do I have the faith to manifest this week?

WRITE. New car + loan. I'm struggling with the fear of no amount of money ever being enough for me and my son to be taken care of.

SHIFT. I'm grateful that I just worked out the "good, better, best" numbers. It helps me know what I need to survive and thrive.

If I had tackled my fears I would feel calm, confident and wouldn't be financially dependent on anyone. I would have a new car, a new bathroom, and would hire someone to help me organize the house and pantry. I would be able to pay everyone and the support I need and want.

SCRIPT. *I'm so excited I hit six figures in July! God and I are more connected than ever. I'm so happy I made journaling a part of my daily routine. I love my workout regimen and showering/taking a hot bath in my new soaking tub. It's such an energizing and relaxing routine.*

I feel my absolute best and most fit ever. I'm the calmest I've ever been.

At face value it might seem as though what Taryn wrote didn't really have anything to do with what she manifested. Aside from the fact that she wrote "New car + loan" at the very beginning. But if you go back to the journal prompt, the question was, "What do I have the faith to manifest this week?" As soon as she answered that question, her subconscious mind understood the assignment: Feed Taryn thoughts that propel her into action for the car and loan. Taryn herself wrote in our community post that she was doing *her* part.

One thing about Taryn is that she's going to do her part. She shows up to all of our group coaching calls, she journals just about every single day, if she needs support she asks for it. Taryn has taken total accountability and responsibility for her part in getting results and it shows.

That's what the Faith Activated Journal Method is all about— you getting clear on what you want (now and in the future) and then doing your part to help bring forth the manifestation.

I gotta tell ya, I love this work so much that sharing just these three examples made me think of how cool it would be to have an entire book filled with journal entries and the manifestations produced as a result of making this method a daily habit. Who knows, maybe that'll be my next book. For now, instead of reading about what other people did, how about you give it a try yourself?

Here are seven journal prompts to help you get started. Remember the cyclical steps of the Faith Activated Journal Method: *Write,*

Shift, Script. Feel free to go back and forth through each step as needed. Do your best to get to the *Script.* That's where the mind really gets a chance to help unlock the manifestation.

> DAY 1: *What do I want more of and what's stopping me from having it?*
>
> DAY 2: *What is my vision for the next twelve months of my life?*
>
> DAY 3: *What step will I take today to create more freedom?*
>
> DAY 4: *Who do I need to become in order to live with more faith and truth?*
>
> DAY 5: *What doubt or disbelief am I holding on to when it comes to getting more of what I want?*
>
> DAY 6: *Where have I held back my truth and what happens when I start to live more in my truth?*
>
> DAY 7: *What do I fear most about living a permission to offend lifestyle and what if those fears weren't true?*

Sometimes this work can be quite challenging, especially the *Script.* The key to mastering the *Script* is to pay attention to the doubt, fear, or disbelief that might try to pop in. If you feel any of that, instead of trying to "force" the *Script,* go back to the *Write* and get curious about those intrusive thoughts. Again, this takes practice, but keep trying. You'll get the hang of it!

To get more journal prompts, head over to RachelLuna.biz/offend to access all the extras I've created for you.

Great job! Meet me over in chapter 12 to read some pretty cool stories of Offense in Action.

12

OFFENSE IN ACTION

The following stories are examples of how real people, just like you, have applied the tools in this book and given themselves permission to offend. After each story, I'll point out some of the strategies being implemented from the book and which chapter to refer to should you find yourself in a similar situation. I hope that as you read their stories you are inspired to take confident action and create your own stories of "offense in action."

The Customer Isn't Always Right
ANNE'S STORY

After spending more than a week of back-and-forth messages on social media, giving a *ton* of free advice, and holding space for a woman who was ready to invest thousands of dollars to work with me, I told her *not* to join my program. The woman had already invested nearly $30,000 in a business that was stagnant. Although it isn't always true for everyone, I could tell that for this woman, another big investment would crush her, not help her.

Because I believe in using situations like these as teachable moments, I wrote an email to my audience describing how I had suggested this woman not join my program. I also shared my philosophies on how my industry often sells out of desperation and shared some other tidbits. I didn't use any identifiable markers that would tip anyone off as to who this woman was.

Her first message to me after she read my email was, *"That was a little less than encouraging."* I quickly responded with, *"Hey, I didn't mean for it to feel that way. I apologize if it was discouraging to you. Honestly, I'm frustrated for you because this is how the industry is and it needs a major overhaul. I'm sure your story is going to help people someday, and I'm really sorry you're going through this."*

"This" being the fact that she had just paid $5,000 for someone to set up a project management system for her in a business that wasn't generating the revenue she needed. I had been so nice to her in every exchange. So I was really surprised when she sent me a long message accusing me of breeching her trust. Among other things she wrote, *"What I don't appreciate is you sharing my story (or anybody's story) publicly, especially when they're going through it and in the trenches, to use for your sales benefit . . . I'm sorry I entrusted you with where I'm at. I hope this doesn't happen to others and I hope this isn't a tactic taught to your clients either."*

I was dumbfounded! Not only had I not used her name, age, business, or anything else to identify her in my email, but also it wasn't just *her* story to tell. It was my story too! I had given this woman a week of my time and energy and offered her lots of free advice. She was ready to buy my mastermind [program] and every course I have, and I made her take all of her stuff out of her cart, and now she was making me out to be some coach capitalist who was taking advantage of her!

There was no way I could let this slide. I took a few moments to gather my thoughts and drop into my heart. I was determined to stand up for myself. I wrote back, *"I hear you and can see your perspective, and I don't* share your opinion. I am sorry you felt hurt by the email. I mean that. It came from a place of love.

"I don't agree that I breeched confidentiality. I did not use any identifying markers that would suggest who I was speaking about.

"You were interested in spending thousands with me and I told you not to. I operate my business out of integrity and I stand by that 100 percent and I shared that story because I hope more people will operate their business this way.

"Between the week of back and forth, listening to you, holding space for you, giving you free advice and refusing to take your money, I stand by my actions."

Standing up for myself felt empowering and authentic to who I am. I'm sharing this story here because it is my story to share. Period. End of story.

What I love about Anne's story is how she was able to acknowledge what the prospective client was saying *without* giving in or taking inappropriate responsibility for any wrongdoing. You can see how Anne was operating from her Empathetic Offender identity. If you want to engage in productive conversations like the one Anne had, you can flip back to chapter 1 and practice using the Framework for Freedom. Next time you're faced with a difficult situation, run it through the framework, tap into *your truth*, and respond with confidence and empathy.

Standing Your Ground
ANDREA'S STORY

The contractor that I was using had been making some decisions thinking that he had spoken to me and he hadn't. He told me that I had forgotten to tell him that we were installing LED mirrors in the master so the electrical wasn't ready despite the fact that the vision boards I had sent him included the LED mirrors down to the wattage of the bulb.

Then he said I didn't tell him I wanted three lights in the guest bedroom and he only installed two. He asked me about that and I told him there was no way because my entire Pinterest vision board showed three lights. So I was making my vision work around what he had already done so that he wouldn't have to do more work. Then he put in the shower shelf. I wanted a beautiful crisp white shower wall with gold fixtures. He ended up installing a shower shelf with a stone material I had not approved. When I walked in and saw the work, the shelf looked yellow. But it was already installed to include the grout. This wasn't what I had ordered—at all.

We spoke and he essentially said, *"There's nothing we can do now,"* and I remember just trying to calm down. I walked back to my office and I thought to myself, *You know what—that's not true. I conceded before when he had installed the lights in the bathroom and the electrical in all the wrong places. I had shifted my plans according to what he had done even though that wasn't my desire for the renovation.*

I sat with myself for a moment and said, *The truth is, we can pull all the tiles and shelf out, and it can be replaced and re-grouted. That shelf can come out. And that shelf **is** coming out because there's no way that I'm going to walk into the dream renovation that I've been saving for and planning over the past three years as I've been living in this fixer-upper to look at that shower shelf and feel unsatisfied and regret never speaking up for myself.*

So I walked back in and said, *"You may not like this, but that shelf needs to come out."* The tile guy looked at the grout guy and said, *"The lady said it's coming out."* My GM [general contract manager] scoffed in frustration and said, *"Well, uh, what do you want to replace it with?"*

"Match it to what you used in the window sill. That's perfect." I responded. And it was done.

It sounded like it was this big issue when in truth it only took a few hours to fix. But they made it seem like the shelf was set in stone until I said it wasn't and I said, "This is my vision. This is what I want." I could feel the density in my stomach trying to accept the thought of *I don't get to have what I want even though I'm paying premium price.*

I felt bad at first, asking for them to redo the work, and had to resolve that within myself, because I don't like to cause people extra work. I had to reframe that for myself and say, *Actually I haven't caused anyone extra work. The GM caused extra work, and that's not on me. And they absolutely have a responsibility to fix this because that material was never approved by the owner—that's me! I'm the owner, designer, and ultimately the person that should walk into that room every single day and feel madly in love with the design.*

And they fixed it. And now I walk into that room and I'm madly in love—as I should be!

I can relate to Andrea's story so much because there have been countless times in my life when I settled for less than what I wanted because I didn't want to burden others. Can you relate? The next time you're faced with a situation in which you think you might be adding more work for someone or inconveniencing another person, refer back to chapter 7 and use the alignment opportunity to work through the All Outcomes Matrix.

When Andrea was sitting in her office reflecting on what the GM had told her, she was working though the All Outcomes Matrix. Thinking about the worst-case scenario—walking into a bathroom and feeling regret every single day—was exactly what she needed to help her stand up for herself and her true desires. Today, Andrea *loves* her bathroom, but more than that, she's one of the most gentle Empathetic Offenders I know, and it's beautiful to behold! I'm excited for the same to be true for you.

Blood Is Not Thicker than Boundaries
DIONNE'S STORY

For the longest time I struggled with my relationship with my sister. Growing up, she bullied me, beat me, and teased me. Her abuse is one of the reasons I developed such poor self-image issues. I'm still working on these issues.

After not speaking to me for several years, she suddenly decided she wanted a relationship with me. She wanted to visit my home and stay a few days. But she's never apologized to me for how she hurt me. I must have peace in my home. When she asked to come visit, I had to say no. I gave myself permission to offend and told her I would not tolerate her coming to my home, talking about my weight, teasing me, and expecting me to be okay with that kind of behavior.

Out of respect for our mother I speak to my sister on the phone, but I do not entertain any of her other requests. My peace is more important. I am worthy of living a peaceful, abuse-free life.

Although the story Dionne submitted was short and sweet, it didn't end there. She continued to work through many of the alignment opportunities, and in particular, she has made the Faith Activated Journaling Method from chapter 9 a part of her daily routine. Through her journaling practice, Dionne has manifested new business deals, media coverage, and over $17,500 in business grants. Dionne's company was recently named Minority Business of the Year in her hometown, and best of all, Dionne's sister apologized to her and they even hugged at the end of the exchange. This was a *huge* breakthrough, but her wins didn't stop there. You see, once Dionne gave herself permission to offend, she was able to start scripting a new story for her life.

Dionne recently joined me at one of my mastermind retreats, and on the last day she stood before us and said, "I can now look in the mirror and not call myself ugly." Of all the breakthroughs I've watched Dionne experience, that last one was the most powerful, in my opinion. For years her poor self-image had stopped her from showing up in many areas of her life. From relationships to business, Dionne had been hiding out. But as she worked through the Framework for Freedom (in chapter 1), increased her Offense Capacity Quotient (in chapter 5), used the Faith Activated Journaling Method almost daily (in chapter 9), and gave herself permission to offend, Dionne was able to turn the key and set herself free. So can you.

The Jaw Dropper
VICTORIA'S STORY

After spending more than fifteen years in corporate, I decided to bet on myself and become a full-time entrepreneur. When I started, I had no idea what I was doing. I didn't know how I was going to create a consistent income or where my next check would come from. What I did know was that I was going to hustle my ass off and figure it out as I went.

Within my first six months, I had the opportunity to lock in a big contract with the largest asset manager in the world. I was super excited and had a plan to ask for $125,000 for a five-month engagement. I thought that was fair and a lot of money, especially for my first big contract.

As I prepped for the negotiation process, I reached out to a mentor who had been in the consulting game for over twenty years. When I told him how much I was going to ask for, he challenged me. He wanted to know why I was asking for such a low number. He said I needed to think bigger and stop thinking like a rookie. At first, I was taken aback because $125,000 was a lot of money. I deserved that money, but clearly I was new to the game and needed to listen and learn. I put my limiting beliefs to the side and took notes. I ended up locking in that contract for $175,000.

It was at that moment that I decided I was going to give myself permission to offend. I was going to ask for the most, do the most, and live the most. I was going to drop jaws with my asking price. I was going to own it, and not be discouraged if someone could not afford me. I was no longer going to take other people's discomfort and make it my own. I'm exclusive—a luxury brand, that does not go on sale.

If Victoria's story isn't the perfect way to wrap up this section, I don't know what story would be. In person, Victoria is exactly as you might imagine her to be. She is bold, sassy, loud, and hard charging. One thing I deeply admire about Victoria is her ability to *ask*. Regardless of what others might think, Victoria will ask you for the sun, moon, stars, and a bottle of champagne on the side—with expectation! And guess what? More often than not *she gets what she wants!*

If you want to start boldly asking for and getting more of what you want, just like Victoria, revisit chapter 2, where you can practice defining your beliefs + values, and then, if you haven't already, complete the alignment opportunities in chapter 3 to anchor in your identity.

I hope you can see that this entire book has been structured to be a valuable resource for present and future use. Come back to it often.

Flip through the sections based on whatever is going on in your life. And for added support, consider joining us in the Ready to Offend Challenge.

READY TO OFFEND CHALLENGE

As you begin to walk in the Empathetic Offender identity, I want to make sure you are fully supported. Now more than ever the world needs people like you to take a warrior stance for love, unity, and acceptance. That's why I want to personally invite you to become a member of the #loyalLUNAtics community and join our Ready to Offend Challenge.

Let me explain. The #loyalLUNAtics are my friends and community members. We have big dreams and goals, and we're crazy enough to believe they can and will come true. Our Ready to Offend Challenge is the next step toward leading with empathy while standing in your truth. The good news is that you don't have to stand alone. You get to rise up in empathetic offense alongside a supportive community. Whether you're giving yourself permission to speak up, to show up more boldly, or to be the person in your family who breaks the curse of generational poverty and creates financial independence, we get to do this *together*.

Sign up for all the extra resources my team and I have compiled for you over at PermissiontoOffend.com/more. There, you'll get journal prompts, action steps, and more to help you put everything you've learned into practice. It's totally free and it's waiting for you now. I'll meet you there.

ACKNOWLEDGMENTS

If you're like me, you're probably reading this page first. I always enjoy seeing who is part of the community that brings a book to life. And *you*, my dear, have made that possible. Thank you for being here. Excuse me just a moment while I acknowledge a few other people who helped make this book possible.

God, I thank you first, even though I wrote this last. Thank you for sending your son, Jesus Christ—the OG offender who showed us all how to live unfiltered, unashamed, and unafraid—to die for me. Thank you for delivering me from cancer and for allowing this dream to become a reality. Thank you for keeping me covered through every storm of life. Thank you, Lord, for all of it.

To my daughters, Isabella and Valentina—my God, I love you both so much. I dedicated this book to you, and now I want to acknowledge the major role you've each played in helping this book as well as so many of my other dreams come to life. I would not be who or where I am today without the lessons I've learned being your mama. Thank you, my sweet little bun-buns. Thank you for always encouraging me to keep going when I wanted to stop writing. Thank you both for all the time you've allowed me to spend writing this book instead of being present with you. I know in my heart of hearts that your sacrifice will help someone else's life be transformed as they read this book. You, Valentina, you, Isabella, are transformers, and you've already changed the world simply because you're in it. I love you forever, no matter what.

To my husband, Dakar, thank you for believing in *me* even when you didn't fully believe in the vision I held for my dreams. Thank you for believing in Confidence Activated and for betting on me even when I was playing with a losing hand. Thank you for never letting go of the vision you had for me as an author and for the one millllionnnn dollars (still working on that one. LOL). You are more than words. I love you forever, no matter what.

To my mother, Carmen Santini—my mommy, *mima*, the wind beneath my wings. You literally saved my life. You are the reason she let me live, and I could never, ever return to you all that you've given me. Thank you for all of your sacrifices. Thank you for letting me share the stories I shared in this book from *my* perspective. You have been and continue to be the most wonderful, loving mother I could have ever asked for. Thank you for being my confidante and for teaching me how to pray and love the Lord. I love you.

To my inner, most inner circle—Best Friend (Melisa Miranda) and Celita—I don't think I could do life without the two of you. Maybe that sounds like I'm being extra, but oh well—I'm extra, and it's true. You've been by my side through the best and worst seasons of my life. You each have held me up when all I wanted to do was lay it all down. No matter what was going on in your own lives, you've each always made my life a priority, and for that, there will never be enough words. Thank you for believing in me even when I didn't believe in myself. I love you both.

Speaking of people who made this book possible, I must start by thanking my friend Lauren Messiah. Thank you for giving me the verbal kick in the butt to get going on this project, for talking me off the emotional ledge more times than I can count, for 6 a.m. text messages, and for never cosigning on my lazy fashion choices. Love ya, girl!

Thank you, Andrea Owen, for being so generous with your time when talking me through the entire process, encouraging me, and introducing me to the best agent on the planet. I am beyond grateful.

To Michele Martin, my incredible agent, THANK YOU! THANK YOU! THANK YOU! Yes, you get extra thanks and all caps. Thank you for believing in me and this book. Thank you for your wonderful guidance, encouragement, and advocacy. I adore you and am so honored to call you *my* agent! (P.S. Did I ever tell you that I had written your name in my journal years ago and declared you would one day be my agent? Look at us now. True story.) ☺

To Judith Curr and Hilary Swanson, thank you for saying yes to this book. To Aidan Mahoney, you were one of the reasons I said yes back. Thank you for your early feedback on this manuscript. It helped me tremendously. To Edward Benitez, *mil gracias por tu apoyo en lanzar este libro en colaboración con* HarperCollins Español. *Tu entusiasmo para este proyecto me apoyó más de lo que te imaginas. ¡¡Gracias, Edward!!*

To my sweet, kind, and brilliant editor, Sydney Rogers. We did it!! Thank you for giving this manuscript so much love, attention, and detailed feedback, even when you were swamped with a bajillion other irons in the fire. You made this book better, and I'm so grateful I got *you*.

To the entire team at HarperOne and HarperCollins Español: THANK YOU!!! This has been an incredible experience, and I'm so grateful to have been able to partner with such a fantastic house. I won!

To my writing coach, Candice Davis: you are more than words. Thank you for being my coach, friend, confidante, and sometimes therapist (ha!). Thank you for pushing me to go deeper and for pulling out the goodness that was hidden under my own layers of fear. Your commitment to this movement is why this book is here now.

To my friends who are truly inspiring mentors—ladies, you are the women God sent when I journaled and prayed for people of influence to work on my behalf and support my endeavors. Eternal gratitude for each one of you:

Tiphani Montgomery, you were the first person to teach me to pray for people of influence to work on my behalf. You were the one who taught me to take a bold stand for God, no matter what. Thank you for every word of life you spoke over me, for fasting for me when I was too sick to fast for myself, for being such a wonderful teacher for me when it came to raising my own OCQ. For all of that and so much more, *thank you.*

Patrice Washington, you have been my prayer partner, my confidante, and an ever-present friend indeed. Thank you for nearly a decade of love, support, and collaboration.

Lori Harder, from the moment we met you have poured into me without ever asking or expecting anything in return. This matters more than you know because one of my stories growing up was "People only ever want to take from me." But you came into my life, and all you've ever done is give generously of your time, your talent, and even your money. Thank you! You helped break a story and set me free! I love you, friend!

Marshawn Evans Daniels, thank you for *always* being available for me no matter what, when, where, or why. Thank you for your wisdom, guidance, friendship, and sisterhood. I love you and I'm so grateful to you!

Jamie Kern Lima—*Jamie Kern Lima!* (Can you hear me saying it? LOL.) Truly, you were the answer to so many of my prayers. I thank God for using you to change my life. And I thank *you* for being obedient to the call. Jamie, I will never forget all that you've done for me and for all our attendees at Confidence Activated 2021. I promise, your investment in me and them will not fall to the ground. We will all continue to pay forward your kindness, love, and generosity. *I* will continue to show up for others the way you showed up for me. You are the *true* embodiment of women supporting women. (P.S. Thank you so much for my Lia Valencia Key *"Believe"* bracelet and my Crystalynn Aucoin *"Home"* necklace. I wear them every single day as a reminder of how God answers our prayers.)

A very special thank you to my girlfriends who have laughed with me, cried with me, and stood by my side as I weathered through life's storms, you know who you are. Thank you. I love you.

To all the women who lent their stories to this book and to all of the members of The Faith Activated Journaling Experience—your faith is a testimony and I thank you.

To any of my peeps I may have forgotten, please know the ADHD is real and my forgetfulness doesn't reflect my love for you.

To Dr. Max Gerson, Charlotte Gerson, and the entire Gerson family: thank you for helping me heal. To my incredible team of doctors and practitioners—Dr. Beth, Dr. Sarah Wilde, Dr. Matt— thank you for helping save my life.

And to my #loyalLUNAtics, who have dealt with my inconsistency and loved me anyway. You are the reason there's a podcast and emails and events and now books! I promise to keep showing up for you as long as you show up for yourselves! Dream bigger, offend more—I believe in you.

> Beloved, I pray that all may go well with you
> and that you may be in good health,
> as it goes well with your soul.
>
> —3 JOHN 1:2, ESV

ABOUT THE AUTHOR

What else can I tell you that I haven't already shared throughout the pages of this book? You already know one of the most shame-inducing, humiliating experiences of my life (unless you skipped the introduction, in which case you should go back and read that part). You've read about my journey healing through cancer. I've shared some of the ups and downs of my marriage (shout-out to my hubby for letting me put our business on front street). So what else should you know "about the author"?

Well, here's the professional bio. Just in case you're into those flashy accolades.

Rachel Luna is a certified master neuroscience and life coach, international speaker, and host of the top-rated podcast, *Permission to Offend*, where she talks faith, worth, and wealth. *Forbes* rated her one of the "11 Most Inspiring Female Entrepreneurs to Follow on Instagram" (@GirlConfident) and her work, which goes beyond cliches, rah-rah speeches, and platitudes and dives deep into the root of the issue, has been featured in *Success*, *Latina*, and *HuffPost* and on Lifetime.

Born and raised in New York City, Rachel, who calls herself "a magnet for miracles," comes from a life of resilience. Despite losing both her parents to AIDS, struggling with eating disorders in her teens, and battling alcoholism and depression in her early twenties, Rachel has never allowed herself to be limited by life circumstances. Instead, she persevered and when she was diagnosed with triple negative breast cancer in the summer of 2019, Rachel tackled it the same way she does everything—with grit, tenacity, faith, and confidence.

These experiences, along with her decade of service in the United States Marine Corps and tour of duty in Iraq during Operation Enduring Freedom/Operation Iraqi Freedom, have given her the strength and ability to not only handle adversity, but to thrive in it.

As a woman of color, who was repeatedly told to keep her mouth shut, not make waves, and fall in line, Rachel has succeeded in remaining true to herself; speaking up, standing out, and leading the charge to help others do the same. Her courses have helped over three thousand women (and a few fellas) gain clarity, confidence, and massive business growth, many of whom have crossed into six and seven figures with ease. Rachel has helped thousands of people around the world (over ninety countries to be exact) through her weekly podcast episodes, email newsletters, speaking tours, and workshops.

Standing only four feet, eleven inches tall, Rachel is a tiny but mighty firecracker who lights up the room and galvanizes audiences all around the world. A captivating speaker, who brings massive fire and energy to any room she enters, Rachel has been invited to share her powerful talks across the globe including, North America, Europe, and Asia.

Rachel Luna is the coach the "every woman" needs, *yesterday*!

So that's the fancy, fancy bio.

Now let me tell you who I really am . . .

I'm determined, not disciplined. I struggle with ADHD on the regular and consider myself to be an organized mess. I know where everything is, so don't mess with my piles. You won't find more than a few hours pass without me praying, praising, or engaging in a conversation with God. I'm a vegan, green juice–loving, small talk–hating, journal-obsessed life changer. Warning: hanging out with me for too long will cause massive change and transformation in your life, *for the better*!

Who I really am is a woman who couldn't stop doing this work even if she tried. (And I've tried.)

I spend most of my days offending my husband, our two daughters, and our Maltipoo, Layla, in Jacksonville, Florida.

INDEX